Student Companion to

Jane
AUSTEN

Student Companion to

Jane
AUSTEN

Debra Teachman

Student Companions to Classic Writers

Greenwood Press
Westport, Connecticut • London

Library of Congress Cataloging-in-Publication Data

Teachman, Debra, 1955–
    Student companion to Jane Austen / Debra Teachman.
       p. cm.—(Student companions to classic writers, ISSN 1522–7979)
    Includes bibliographical references (p.) and index.
    ISBN 0–313–30747–4 (alk. paper)
    1. Austen, Jane, 1775–1817—Criticism and interpretation.   2. Women and
literature—England—History—19th century.   I. Title. II. Series.
PR4036.T38   2000
823.′7—dc21   99–058877

British Library Cataloguing in Publication Data is available.

Library of Congress Catalog Card Number: 99–058877
ISBN: 0–313–30747–4
ISSN: 1522–7979

First published in 2000

Greenwood Press, 88 Post Road West, Westport, CT 06881
An imprint of Greenwood Publishing Group, Inc.
www.greenwood.com

Printed in the United States of America

The paper used in this book complies with the
Permanent Paper Standard issued by the National
Information Standards Organization (Z39.48–1984).

10 9 8 7 6 5 4 3 2 1

Contents

Series Foreword

This series has been designed to meet the needs of students and general readers for accessible literary criticism on the American and world writers most frequently studied and read in the secondary school, community college, and four-year college classrooms. Unlike other works of literary criticism that are written for the specialist and graduate student, or that feature a variety of reprinted scholarly essays on sometimes obscure aspects of the writer's work, the Student Companions to Classic Writers series is carefully crafted to examine each writer's major works fully and in a systematic way, at the level of the nonspecialist and general reader. The objective is to enable the reader to gain a deeper understanding of the work and to apply critical thinking skills to the act of reading. The proven format for the volumes in this series was developed by an advisory board of teachers and librarians for a successful series published by Greenwood Press, Critical Companions to Popular Contemporary Writers. Responding to their request for easy-to-use and yet challenging literary criticism for students and adult library patrons, Greenwood Press developed a systematic format that is not intimidating but helps the reader to develop the ability to analyze literature.

How does this work? Each volume in the Student Companions to Classic Writers series is written by a subject specialist, an academic who understands students' needs for basic and yet challenging examination of the writer's canon. Each volume begins with a biographical chapter, drawn from published sources, biographies, and autobiographies, that relates the writer's life to his or her work. The next chapter examines the writer's literary heritage, tracing the literary influences of other writers on that writer and explaining and discussing the literary genres into which the writer's work falls. Each of the following chapters examines one or more major works by the writer, featuring those works most frequently read and studied by high school and college students. Depending on the writer's canon, generally between four and eight major works are examined, each in an individual chapter. The discussion of each work is organized into separate sections on plot development, character development, and major themes. Literary devices and style, narrative point of view, and historical setting are also discussed in turn if pertinent to the work. Each chapter concludes with an alternate critical perspective from which to read the works, such as psychological or feminist criticism. The critical theory is defined briefly in easy, comprehensible language for the student. Looking at the literature from the point of view of a particular critical approach will help the reader to understand and apply critical theory to the act of reading and analyzing literature.

Of particular value in each volume is the bibliography, which includes a complete bibliography of the writer's major works, a selected bibliography of biographical and critical works suitable for students, and lists of reviews of each work examined in the companion, all of which will be helpful to readers, teachers, and librarians who would like to consult additional sources.

As a source of literary criticism for the student or for the general reader, this series will help the reader to gain understanding of the writer's work and skill in critical reading.

1

The Life of Jane Austen

Jane Austen is often depicted as a very quiet spinster, growing up in a small country town with her father as rector of a simple country church. Her novels are often considered to focus only on the lives of a few individuals in a few families living, for the most part, in rather confined and conservative country towns. The first published full-length biography of Jane Austen contributed greatly to the establishment of this view of her life and her novels. Her nephew, James Edward Austen-Leigh published *A Memoir of Jane Austen* in 1870 (with a second, enlarged edition appearing in 1871). "Of events," her nephew wrote, "her life was singularly barren: few changes and no great crisis ever broke the smooth current of its course. Even her fame may be said to have been posthumous: it did not attain to any vigorous life till she had ceased to exist" (1–2). This *Memoir*, written and published over fifty years after his famous aunt's death, described a simple, respectable woman whose family always came first and whose gentility never allowed her to "meddle with matters which she did not thoroughly understand" within the pages of her novels as well as her life (13). Austen-Leigh's relief that his aunt's novels did not deal (overtly, at least) with such serious subjects as politics, law, war, or international events is clear throughout the *Memoir*. His Victorian bias against respectable women being involved in writing and publishing novels that discuss important social and legal concepts is evident in his fifty-year-old memory of his aunt. As a result of that bias, Austen-Leigh appears to have softened the rather rough and caustic edges of his famous aunt's personality. By portraying her as the ultimate respectable Victorian lady, he made her life palatable to his contemporaries, but he dulled the edges of her personality and wit considerably—as can be seen by reading her letters as well as those of friends and relatives who wrote about her. He has also minimized some of the more significant and interesting events that did, indeed, occur to her and her family. In the *Memoir*, he created a somewhat falsified image of his aunt that has remained her dominant public image for nearly two hundred years.

Nevertheless the *Memoir* is a very useful book in many ways. It provides its readers with a vision of Jane Austen from a family member who knew her when he was a child. It also allows us to see life in Georgian England from the perspective of a very observant man who was a talented writer of his observations, a talent he shared with his famous aunt. But as a biography of the woman and author Jane Austen, the *Memoir* is incomplete. It revises and omits many of the details of her life that are most interesting to readers of her novels two centuries after she lived.

Jane Austen was born on December 16, 1776, in Steventon, a small town in Hampshire, England. Her father was a clergyman, rector of the two small country parishes of Steventon and Deane. The seventh of eight children (six sons and two daughters), Jane Austen was raised in the midst of a lively, intelligent, and successful household. Her father was a very well-respected clergyman and scholar. Two of her brothers ultimately became admirals in the Navy under the famous British naval commander Horatio Nelson, one became a successful clergyman, another ended his career as a clergyman after rather checkered and complicated careers in the militia and in banking, and yet another brother, adopted by aristocratic cousins who had no children of their own, eventually owned and managed great country estates in the English countryside.

Austen knew and appreciated small-town life in the English countryside, but she also understood and sometimes enjoyed the social life of London, of the aristocratic great country houses of England, and of various English resort towns such as Bath and Brighton. Her novels tend to be set predominantly in small towns and villages in the English countryside, but her characters travel to London, Bath, Brighton, and even such distant lands as British India and the island of Antiqua in the West Indies, lands she knew much of from tales of the travels of her own family members. Although she does not include scenes that overtly depict scenes of political intrigue, war, or colonial activity, her characters' lives reflect an England involved in all three. Austen's novels may appear on the surface to deal only with the lives of a few country families in small country towns, but upon close examination, all aspects of English life are included in the details.

Jane Austen's father, the Reverend George Austen, came from a family that proudly traced its ancestry back to the Middle Ages, and its ownership of land

and, thus, political power, to the sixteenth century. George Austen was the son of a surgeon, William, in a branch of the Austen family that was not wealthy. His parents died, however, when he was only six years old, leaving him in the care of his uncle Francis Austen, a man of considerable wealth and power. Francis Austen provided very well for his young nephew's education, sending him to Tonbridge Grammar School and then to St. John's College at Oxford. Such provision for an orphaned, impoverished nephew was not the norm, but it was also not entirely uncharacteristic of eighteenth-century landowners. Such men often would "adopt" the sons of poorer relatives (sometimes legally, sometimes implicitly) in order to make certain that less affluent branches of the family be financially provided for and that the family property stay intact and cared for within the family.

Once George graduated from St. John's College at Oxford, he began a career in teaching, first holding a position at Tonbridge, where he himself had attended school, then becoming a teaching Fellow at St. John's College. In 1760, he took holy orders (became ordained) in the Anglican Church, enabling him to become a clergyman/scholar, the Reverend George Austen. Taking holy orders made him eligible to accept the position of rector at the small country churches of Steventon and Deane, positions soon to be offered him by wealthier relatives.

In 1764, four years after taking holy orders, the Reverend George Austen, age 32, married Cassandra Leigh, age 24, in the resort town of Bath. Cassandra Leigh, like George Austen, had an ancestry of which she was quite proud. Her father was a clergyman/scholar who had been a Fellow of All Saints at Oxford. Her uncle was the legendary Dr. Leigh, Master of Balliol College, a man known and respected throughout England for his intelligence, wit, and charm. Cassandra's ancestors included Sir Thomas Leigh, who had been Lord Mayor of London during the reign of Queen Elizabeth I, and his son, who had sheltered Charles I at Stoneleigh Abbey during the English Civil War. Cassandra and George both had good reasons to be proud of their biological and cultural heritage.

After their marriage, the Reverend George and Cassandra Leigh Austen moved to Hampshire, England where George's relatives had provided them with two parishes of which George could be rector. In the eighteenth century, the positions of rectors (ministers) of Anglican churches were determined by the process of granting a "living." The living, that is rectorship of the local church, in a community was essentially the property of someone, usually a major landowner in the area. The owner of the living could then grant or sell the position to a duly ordained clergyman of the Anglican Church. Thus, the rector of the village church was chosen, not by the community or by the church's hierarchy, but by the person who owned the right to "grant" it.

Two separate wealthy relatives granted George Austen the livings of churches in neighboring parishes. A distant cousin, Thomas Knight of Godmersham in Kent, owned the living at Steventon, which he offered to George, and Francis Austen, George's uncle and primary benefactor since childhood, purchased the living at the neighboring community of Deane which he presented to his nephew as a gift. The total income from the position of rector in both parishes was small by the standards of George Austen's aristocratic relatives, but it was sufficient to support the Austen family, albeit modestly. George Austen added to his income by teaching young gentlemen who came to the rectory to board and be educated by the former Oxford Fellow, and the small family farm that Cassandra supervised provided the family and the resident scholars with dairy products, fresh vegetables, grains, and poultry.

Jane was born in the Steventon rectory where she probably spent the first three or four months of her life with her immediate family. Then, if Jane's infancy ran true to form in the Austen household (and there is no reason to suppose it did not), she was taken in by a woman in the village to be looked after for another year and a half or so, to be returned home only after she had grown to the point where she would not be too difficult to handle. This fostering of infants was the system of infant-rearing that Mrs. Austen, along with many other middle- and upper-class women of the time, believed best suited both infant and family. At the time, the idea that infants might have any psychological bond with their caretakers before they were capable of speech or walking was inconceivable to most parents. They did not believe that they could be harming their children in any way by sending them away for as much as two of their first three years, so long as they chose the foster family with care. The Austen family obviously did choose their fostering families with care, as all eight of their children survived into adulthood, a major triumph in late-eighteenth-century England when the mortality rate for infants was extremely high.

Following the period of time during which Jane was probably fostered in the village, she would have been returned to Steventon where she spent much of her early life within the walls and surrounding countryside of the rectory. In the Memoir, James Edward Austen-Leigh recounts his memories of the grounds of his aunt's first home:

[I]t presents no grand or extensive views; but the features are small rather than plain. The surface continually swells and sinks, but the hills are not bold, nor the valleys deep; and though it is sufficiently well clothed with woods and hedgerows, yet the poverty of the soil in some places prevents the timber from attaining a large size. Still it has its beauties. The lanes wind along in a natural curve, continually fringed with irregular borders of native turf and lead to pleasant nooks and corners. . . .

A hedgerow, in that country, does not mean a thin formal line of quickset, but an irregular border of copsewood and timber, often wide enough to contain within it a winding footpath, or a rough cart track. Under its shelter the earliest primroses, anemones, and wild hyacinths were to be found, sometimes, the first bird's nest; and now and then, the unwelcome adder. Two such hedgerows radiated, as it were, from the parsonage garden. One a continuation of the turf terrace, proceeded westward, forming the southern boundary of the home meadows; and was formed into a rustic shrubbery, with occasional seats, entitled "the Wood Walk." (19–21)

The countryside surrounding Steventon as it is described by Austen-Leigh is quite recognizable to the readers of Austen's novels. Many of her outdoor scenes, especially those involving the developing relationships of young lovers such as Elizabeth Bennett and Fitzwilliam Darcy in *Pride and Prejudice*, take place in gardens and walkways very similar to the grounds of Steventon. Jane's enjoyment of such landscapes is clear in her uses of them in her novels.

The rectory at Steventon was itself little more than a cottage, and one that must have seemed extremely small when filled with Reverend Austen's students as well as his own large family. Jane's literary nephew was used to a significantly higher standard of living than his aunt had been, as well as having become accustomed to the more elaborate and ornate style of the Victorian period. As a result, he wrote about his Aunt Jane's childhood home in less than flattering terms: "[T]he rooms were finished with less elegance than would now be found in the most ordinary dwellings. No cornice marked the junction of wall and ceiling; while the beams which supported the upper floors projected into the rooms below in all their naked simplicity, covered only by a coat of paint or whitewash" (19–20). Jane's niece, Anna, however, remembered the rectory with considerably more affection. Her reflections give insight into the workings of the household as well as the appearance of the rectory:

The dining- or common sitting-room looked to the front and was lighted by two casement windows. On the same side the front door opened into a smaller parlour, and visitors, who were few and rare, were not a bit the less welcome to my grandmother because they found her sitting there busily engaged with her needle, making and mending. In later times . . . a sitting-room was made upstairs: 'the dressing-room,' as they were pleased to call it, perhaps because it opened into a smaller chamber in which my two aunts slept. I remember the common-looking carpet with its chocolate ground, and painted press with shelves above for books, and Jane's piano, and an oval looking glass that hung between the windows. (Hill 30–31)

Anna's description of her aunt's earliest home emphasizes the coziness and functionality of the cottage. She does not describe it as spacious or fashionable;

it was neither. Instead, her description is of a home that was comfortable despite being small and in which the inhabitants could enjoy simple, fulfilling lives.

Most of Jane's earliest years were spent at the Steventon rectory with her parents, all of her brothers but one (her brother George was apparently born with severe physical problems and had to be nursed elsewhere throughout his lifetime), and her sister Cassandra, who was her constant companion. Cassandra was almost three years older than Jane, but there was little that Cassandra could or would do that Jane was not determined to do as well. When it was decided that Cassandra would go to a girls' boarding school along with her older cousin, Jane Cooper, the young Jane Austen went too. Her mother commented on the inseparability of the sisters: "If Cassandra were going to have her head cut off, Jane would insist on sharing her fate" (Le Faye 420).

Jane and Cassandra, along with cousin Jane Cooper, left for Oxford in 1782 to attend school at the home of Mrs. Cawley, the widow of a principal of Brasenose College. Their stay in Oxford was short, however. The school was moved from Oxford to Southampton in 1783, and the three girls moved with it. The Austens appear not to have had any concerns about the relocation of the school at the time. But Southampton was a naval town, and serious illnesses came to the port town soon after the school was moved there. The infection invaded the school, causing all three of the young girls to become ill. The headmistress, perhaps concerned about losing her livelihood, failed to inform her students' parents of the danger of epidemic in both town and school. Fortunately, Jane Cooper was wise enough to write home about the severe health problems at the school when she and both her cousins caught the infection. As a result of her prompt action, Jane Austen was the only one of the three to become seriously ill. As soon as their mothers learned of the illnesses, they both hurried to Southampton to rescue their daughters. The three girls were taken from Southampton in time, but Jane Austen's Aunt Cooper caught the infection from her daughter and died of it.

After a short interval at home in Steventon, Jane and Cassandra were sent to another school. This time they went to the Abbey School at Reading. This school was not known for high academic standards (academics were not considered to be important for girls at this time), but it was recognized as having a very healthy environment and being very well run. The girls remained at the Abbey School from 1785 until the spring of 1787, when they returned to Steventon and began what was probably their most important education, at home in the environment created by their father, brothers, and the scholars under their father's tutelage. Jane was encouraged to read from her father's library of over 500 volumes that included Greek and Roman classics, histories, and political treatises as well as the important poetry, philosophy, and novels of the time. In addition, she was encouraged to discuss her reading with others in her family. This informal education exposed her to many ideas and styles of writing that would have been unavailable to most girls of Austen's time and age. It prepared her for her career as a writer more fully than any approved formal education available to girls in this period could have done.

No record remains to indicate the age at which Jane Austen began writing creative works for her family to read and, in the case of plays, to perform. It is clear, however, both from the amount of juvenile writing that was saved by the family and from references in the family letters and papers, that Jane had begun writing by at least her early teens. These writings were intended for the enjoyment of the family and seem never to have been intended for publication They were, however, neatly written into three notebooks at some point in Jane's life and saved. As a result, we do have the juvenilia available in printed form today.

Jane was not the only individual in her immediate family to have literary aspirations. Her eldest brother, James, ten years older than Jane, was the recognized scholar among the siblings. As a fellow at Oxford, he edited *The Loiterer*. Jane's favorite brother, Henry, also wrote for the literary journal during his education at Oxford. And in the next generation, two nieces, Anna Austen Lefroy and Fanny Knight Knatchbull, as well as Austen's nephew, James Edward Austen-Leigh, had dreams of literary accomplishment and wrote towards the goal of publication.

In 1787, three additions were made to the Steventon household. George Austen's sister, Philadelphia, her daughter Eliza, and Eliza's young son Hastings arrived for a prolonged stay. Eliza had been born in India, where her mother had gone to find a husband. Although Philadelphia Austen was considered to be a very attractive and accomplished young lady in British society, she knew that her chances of finding an eligible husband who could provide well for her in England were very small because of her orphaned status and her lack of any income of her own. Therefore, she determined to go to India where the small numbers of English women available for English men to marry made her financial status much less important than it was in England. Soon after her arrival, she married Tysoe Saul Hancock, a surgeon for the East India Trade Company who also indulged in trading in an attempt to make his fortune in the East. At the time of their meeting and marriage, Hancock was forty-two years old to Philadelphia's twenty-one.

In India, Mr. Hancock became a business partner of and close friend to Warren Hastings, a trader for the East India Company who eventually worked his way up to becoming the Governor, first of Bengal, then of all India. When, after eight years of childless marriage, Mrs. Hancock became pregnant and gave birth to a girl, Hastings agreed to be her godfather, and the child was given the name of his own daughter who had died young, Elizabeth. The closeness between Warren Hastings and Philadelphia Hancock (both of them very attractive and much closer in age than Philadelphia was to her husband) caused many rumors about the biological parentage of young Betsy (who chose to be called Eliza in her late teens), but there is no clear evidence that anyone in the Austen or Hancock family gave credence to the rumors. Regardless of Betsy's actual parentage, however, Hastings looked after the girl and her mother, even providing the girl with a fortune of five thousand pounds before the death of her father and an additional five thousand pounds after her father's death left her and mother without additional support.

In *Catharine, or the Bower,* a tale written during Austen's teenage years, Austen seems to use her aunt Philadelphia's experience as the basis for one of her characters.

The eldest daughter had been obliged to accept the offer of one of her cousins to equip her for the East Indies, and tho' infinitely against her inclinations had been necessitated to embrace the only possibility that was offered to her, of a Maintenance; Yet it was *one*, so opposite to all her ideas of Propriety, so contrary to her Wishes, so repugnant to her feelings, that she would almost have preferred Servitude to it, had Choice been allowed her—. Her personal Attractions had gained her a husband as soon as she had arrived at Bengal, and she had now been married nearly a twelve month. Splendidly, yet unhappily married. United to a Man of double her own age, whose disposition was not amiable, and whose Manners were unpleasing, though his Character was respectable. Kitty had heard twice from her freind [sic] since her marriage, but her Letters were always unsatisfactory, and though she did not openly avow her feelings, yet every line proved her to be Unhappy. She spoke with pleasure of nothing, but of those Amusements which they had shared together and which could return no more, and seemed to have no happiness in veiw [sic] but that of returning to England again. (*Catharine* 187–188)

Although family tradition does not support the idea that Philadelphia Hancock had no love for her husband, it was accepted that their marriage was not particularly passionate and that Mrs. Hancock never seemed to mind the long separation from her husband that was required when he returned to work in India, leaving his wife and daughter behind in England. It is quite possible that Jane Austen heard such a story about her aunt's life from her cousin Eliza during some of their long and intimate conversations over the years.

By the time Jane Austen was old enough to become well acquainted with her cousin, Eliza was an exciting and accomplished young woman, experienced in the ways of India and Continental Europe as well as England. Her stories of aristocratic Europe and London and of exotic British India enthralled her cousins at Steventon. Jane, though fourteen years younger than Eliza, grew very close to her more sophisticated cousin. They shared a love of reading aloud and of acting out scenes of their own composition as well as popular plays of the day. The Austen's barn was used for the family theatricals, which seemed to occur with greater frequency while Eliza was at the rectory than at any other time. Austen's extensive knowledge of contemporary plays as well as her use of the family theatrical as a device in *Mansfield Park* may well have had their inspiration in her association with the sophisticated Eliza.

Those who claim that Jane Austen would have had little knowledge of the world outside of England during her childhood must ignore the effect that Eliza's presence had on her and her family. Not only did Eliza have the experiences of India to draw on, but she had married the Comte de Feuillide, an aristocrat of Louis XVI's court. Eliza had spent considerable time in the French Court with her husband before the French Revolution and kept in close touch with events in France after the revolution began. When the unrest leading to the revolution began, de Feuillide stayed in France to protect his family's holdings while insisting that his wife and son return to safety in England. In 1794, during the period known as the "reign of terror," France's revolutionary Committee of Public Safety put de Feuillide's friend, the Marquise de Marlboef, on trial for knowingly contributing to famine by growing hay for cattle rather than corn or grain for people. De Feuillide tried to help his friend by attempting to bribe witnesses. He was arrested, tried, and found guilty. He was guillotined on the same day as his friend, the Marquise. Eliza was devastated and the entire Austen family horrified. In fact, family legend reports that after de Feuillide's execution, Jane Austen could never again hear the name of France without shuddering. Through Eliza, news of the revolution and the reign of terror were very much present in the Austen household. Jane Austen chose not to put specific depictions of the French Revolution and the Napoleonic wars into her novels, but there is no doubt that she had very clear and detailed knowledge of those situations through her cousin Eliza and her naval brothers. Nor is there any doubt that her knowledge impacted her novels in subtle ways.

The 1790s also saw the enlargement of the Austen family through multiple marriages. Edward Austen, Jane's second eldest brother, married first. As adopted heir to the Knight fortune and estates, he married Elizabeth Bridges, daughter of Sir Brooke Bridges, who owned considerable property as well as a title. Combining their estates and incomes enabled Edward to become one of the most powerful landowners in his region of England once he had inherited the Knight properties and taken the Knight name. Within a year of Edward's marriage, Jane's eldest brother, James, a curate at Overton, married Anne Mathew, daughter of General Mathew and Lady Jane, daughter of the second Duke of Ancaster. Anne Mathew Austen died in 1795, leaving behind a daughter, Anna, born in 1793. In 1797, James remarried, choosing as his second wife

Mary Lloyd, a friend of his sisters Jane and Cassandra. Yet another brother, Henry Thomas Austen, who was at that time a banker, married his widowed cousin Eliza de Feuillide, whom he had loved and admired since childhood. Their marriage took place in 1797, three years after the execution of her first husband in the French Revolution. Eliza, ten years older than her husband, seems to have been a good wife to Henry and to have enjoyed being in even closer relation to her aunt, uncle, and younger cousins. Henry and Eliza spent most of their married life living in style in London, supported by Henry's position in banking and Eliza's financial gifts from her godfather, Warren Hastings. Jane Cooper, a cousin of Jane Austen as well as her close friend since their earliest days, also married in the 1790s, becoming wife to a captain of the Royal Navy in 1792. Due to her parents both being dead, she was married from the rectory at Steventon with members of the Austen family in attendance. The emphasis on courtship and marriage in the Austen home seems to have been at its height during the decade of the 1790s, the same decade during which Jane began writing her most famous novels, also filled with scenes of courtship, romance, and marriage.

In her teenage years, Jane Austen continually experimented with writing. Her earliest writings primarily display her tendency towards satire, as she satirized various events occurring within the family and in the country at large. Twenty-nine pieces of writing from these years were collected by Jane herself, all of which were saved by her family and eventually published in three volumes of juvenilia. In these early writings we can observe Austen's talents as a novelist and satirist developing.

Austen's first and most important audience was her family. Her father presented her with the notebooks in which she collected her writings and was the first person to try (unsuccessfully) to get her writings published. Her mother and siblings listened to her stories and watched short plays she wrote which were produced in the family barn. As her writing progressed and improved, she and her mother often took turns reading her novels to family members and visiting friends (often without revealing the author's identity to the visitors in order to learn their true reactions to the writing as well as to protect the identity of the author). The encouragement provided by these appreciative listeners assisted Austen to grow as a writer, and to quickly develop into a novelist who could enthrall readers of her own generation and continue to attract readers and inspire films to be made of her works two centuries later.

From the earliest days of her serious writing, Austen was determined not to let the secret of her identity be known. She chose to live a quiet life with her family and did not want to experience the kind of public fame that many writers of the time experienced. Her name never appeared on the title page of any of her novels during her lifetime, and she took great care to keep the importance which she gave to her writing secret from all but the closest family members. After the success of her first two novels, her brother Henry became less discreet and, as a point of pride, revealed her identity to so many people that it became an open secret. Jane, nonetheless, continued to behave as though she were not a famous author, refusing, in fact, even to meet other famous authors who indicated a desire to meet her, let alone to associate publicly in literary social events in England.

Although neither Jane nor her sister Cassandra ever married, both indulged themselves in the social life of their community, and both experienced romances of their own. The families with whom the Austen girls did most of their socializing were the Lloyds, the Lefroys, and the Bigg-Withers. The Lloyds and the Lefroys held roughly the same social position as the Austens. The Bigg-Wither family was much more affluent, being a landed family who had inherited the manor house and estate of Manydown. Within these four families, friendships blossomed and romances developed over time.

The Reverend George Lefroy was parson at Ashe, near Steventon and Deane. He and his wife, Anne, were close friends of the Austens. Jane Austen most especially admired the older Anne Lefroy, who often acted as her mentor and guide in a way that her mother never could. Jane and Cassandra frequently visited the Lefroys, both separately and together. The Lefroys and the Austens tended to be invited to the same country parties and balls. George Lefroy's nephew, Tom, from Ireland, visited the Lefroy home in 1795, and Jane and Tom developed a relationship that seems to have been potentially serious. They danced together at local balls and talked long and intimately together, causing rumors about their relationship to start in the community. Such rumors, however, together with the fact that Tom could not have afforded to marry a woman with so little income as Jane, seem to have caused Tom to avoid Jane towards the end of his visit with his aunt and uncle. Upon his return to Ireland, he still seemed to have the possibility of a future with Jane on his mind. He wrote to his aunt that it would give him "particular pleasure to have an opportunity of improving my acquaintance with that family—with a hope of creating to myself a nearer interest. But at present," he clarified, "I cannot indulge any expectation of it" (*Jane Austen's Letters to Her Sister Cassandra and Others* 28). A short time later, he married a woman much more in keeping with his social and financial needs. His career prospered, and he eventually became Lord Chief Justice of Ireland. In his old age, he admitted that he had once "been in love with Jane Austen" but qualified the statement, claiming that "it was a boy's love," puppy love rather than mature love (Austen-Leigh, William 89). In the letters not destroyed by Cassandra after Jane's death, there is only one mention of Tom Lefroy after his departure from Austen's neighborhood, a mention of the fact that she is too proud to ask her friend Mrs. Lefroy about him since his return to Ireland and his marriage.

The degree of Jane's attachment to Tom Lefroy is speculative at best; there was no public recognition of such an attachment beyond a small amount of gossip among friends and acquaintances. Family tradition, however, asserts that Tom was probably the one great love of Jane's life. Cassandra's romantic life, however, was publicly recognized and accepted. In 1796, Cassandra became engaged to the Reverend Thomas Fowle, who had been a student of her father's when he was a boy. Fowle, in order to supplement his income as a clergyman and build a large enough fortune to be able to provide well for Cassandra, served for a time as chaplain to Lord Craven's regiment in the West Indies. What was intended to make his fortune, however, brought about his death. A few weeks before he was to return to England and his beloved Cassandra, Thomas Fowle died of yellow fever. He left his fiancée a legacy of one thousand pounds, which became, in effect, her widow's portion. Cassandra was only twenty-four at the time of her fiancé's death, but she never again seems to have contemplated marriage, or even romance, for herself. She lived to be seventy-two years old.

Jane and Cassandra were very good friends with three young women from the Bigg-Wither family, the prosperous, land-owning family of Manydown House. Throughout their twenties, the young women visited Manydown frequently, meeting much of Hampshire society within its walls and through its associations. The three sisters of the Bigg-Wither family had one brother, a young man by the name of Harris Bigg-Wither. Harris was to inherit a considerable estate as heir to the family fortune. In 1802, when Harris Bigg-Wither was only twenty-one years of age and Jane was almost twenty-seven (the age at which her novels begin to consider her female characters to be spinsters), Harris proposed that Jane become his wife. Although there is no evidence that she had romantic feelings for her friends' brother, she initially accepted the proposal, possibly due to thoughts of the comforts his money and his family could provide. By marrying Harris, Jane would become the wife of the heir to a very large country house and estate in Hampshire. She would be in even closer contact with three of her closest friends, Harris's sisters. She would be able to continue living in the neighborhood of her birth and would be very close to her brother James, who held the living at Steventon after her father's retirement. To marry Harris would enrich her family instead of making her a serious burden, both financially and emotionally, to her father and brothers as years went by. At twenty-seven, she may well have felt that Harris's offer provided her with what was probably her last chance to marry well and have a home of her own. Regardless of her motivations for accepting the proposal, however, by the next morning she had changed her mind. She and Cassandra left Manydown as soon as breakfast was over, after Jane told Harris that her acceptance of his offer had been a mistake. Relations between the Austen and Bigg-Wither families were strained for some time after the event, but the rift was eventually mended, and the women renewed their close friendship.

In 1801, the Reverend George Austen retired from his position as rector of Steventon and Deane, causing the Austen family to leave their beloved home in Steventon and move to the English resort town of Bath. The Austen family already knew Bath well, having vacationed there on numerous occasions. Always before, however, they were visitors, not residents. Jane, in particular, was not pleased with the idea of moving from Steventon to Bath, especially considering the way in which the move was sprung upon her and Cassandra so suddenly. In a letter written in 1869, Jane's niece, Caroline Austen, remembers her mother's discussion of her aunt's reaction:

My Aunt was very sorry to leave her native home, as I have heard my Mother relate. My Aunts had been away a little while, and were met in the Hall on their return by their Mother who told them it was all settled, and they were going to live in Bath. My Mother who was present said my Aunt was greatly distressed. All things were done in a hurry by Mr. Austen. (Wilks 79)

The move to Bath involved more than merely a change of scenery. In order to make the move, Mr. Austen's library of over 500 volumes and all the family furniture had to be sold (the roads being so bad that the furnishings would be unlikely to survive the trip intact). Even Jane's personal pianoforte had to be sacrificed. And Bath was not a quiet country community like Steventon. Instead it was a bustling resort town with 30,000 inhabitants and constant activity. While Bath was a place many people of Austen's time, including Austen herself, enjoyed visiting, it was not the most suitable place for a novelist who needed some degree of peace and quiet for composing books about the lives of those who spend most of their time in the English countryside. From a quiet cottage with its own garden and a shaded walk, the Austens moved to an apartment in a busy town. The change was abrupt and extreme.

Fortunately, Jane had visited Bath on several occasions and understood its ways before the move. She also had family already ensconced in the town. Her grandmother, Mrs. Thomas Leigh had lived in Bath (Jane's own parents had been married in Bath), and her son, James Leigh Perrot and his wife had lived there since 1768. Having family well established in the town made the transition from country to town living much easier for the Austen family than it might otherwise have been. But living in Bath never seems to have set well with the novelist in the family. Her writing patterns were disrupted for the entire time they lived in Bath.

Although Jane never acclimated well to living in the town of Bath, and was unable to write there as well or as consistently as she had at Steventon, her writing seems to have profited from the experience in some ways. Two of her novels, *Northanger Abbey* and *Persuasion*, rely extensively on such resort settings. Her juxtapositions of town life and country life in her novels engage the reader's imagination and enable her to develop characters with much greater depth than might be possible for some of them had they only been depicted in their country lives. Her attention to accurate detail within the novels also was certainly assisted by her time living in Bath. She was able to provide specifics about the intricacies of Bath society in a manner that illuminates personality traits of her characters without heavy-handed exposition on the part of the narrator.

Austen's life in Bath was eventful as well as distressing. Although she did not have the degree of peace and quiet for her writing that she had had at Steventon, she did continue her work. Scholars are uncertain as to whether she began new novels during her time in Bath (the first versions of *Northanger Abbey*, *Sense and Sensibility,* and *Pride and Prejudice*, titled respectively *Susan, Elinor and Marianne,* and *First Impressions*, were written while at Steventon, as was *Mansfield Park*), but Austen seems to have continued revising the novels she had already drafted while at Steventon and began to pursue publication of them in earnest, using a pseudonym to protect her identity, while living in Bath.

In 1803, Jane Austen sold her first novel to a publisher. It was the novel she had titled *Susan*. Messrs. Crosby and Co. bought the novel outright for a sum of ten pounds. The novel was scheduled for publication and even advertised, but for unknown reasons Messrs. Crosby and Co. never published it. Austen eventually arranged to buy the novel back from the publisher and revised it for publication as *Northanger Abbey* some thirteen years after its original sale. What Messrs. Crosby and Co. thought when they discovered that they had neglected to publish and, in fact, had sold back for its original price a novel by the author of the famous and lucrative novels *Sense and Sensibility* and *Pride and Prejudice* can only be imagined. It was certainly not the best business decision they had ever made.

In 1805, four years after moving to Bath, Jane's father died. Not only did Jane, Cassandra, and their mother have their grief to deal with, but they also had to face the significant decrease in income that accompanied the loss of their father and husband. The income remaining after Mr. Austen's death totaled only 210 pounds per year, less than a quarter of what would be required if they were to maintain a lifestyle similar to that they enjoyed with Mr. Austen.

They tried to find less expensive accommodations in Bath, but after a year of living in cheaper, uncomfortable quarters while looking for something more suitable, they determined that they would be better off to move out of Bath. Jane's brothers, Edward, James, and Henry, provided additional income for the Austen women, preventing them from falling into extreme poverty, a fate that often befell unmarried and widowed women of the Austen's social class. Their income remained, however, less than half of what they had while Mr. Austen lived.

In 1806, the Austens left Bath for good. They stayed with various family members and friends and in rented lodgings until 1809, when they moved back to Hampshire into a home of their own at Chawton. This home, known as Chawton Cottage, was owned by Jane's brother Edward as part of the estates he inherited with the Knight properties in Kent. He provided it as a permanent home for his mother, his sisters, and their friend Martha Lloyd, who lived with the Austen women until her marriage to Frank Austen in 1828. The return to Hampshire had a positive effect on Jane's writing and publication. While living in Chawton Cottage, she completed her revisions on her earlier novels and wrote the remainder of them. Her nephew, James Edward Austen-Leigh described in the *Memoir* his experience of his famous aunt's method of composition:

She was careful that her occupation should not be suspected by servants, or visitors, or any persons beyond her own family party. She wrote upon small sheets of paper which could easily be put away, or covered with a piece of blotting paper. There was between the front door and the offices, a swing door which creaked when it was opened; but she objected to having this little inconvenience remedied, because it gave her notice when anyone was coming. (96)

If this secretiveness was, indeed, followed at all times, it must have made Austen's writing process quite cumbersome. Like most of her nephew's insights about his aunt, this one is apt to be somewhat exaggerated. It is clear, however, that Austen was extremely hesitant about revealing herself as an author outside the immediate family and is, therefore, likely that her nephew's account has more than a kernel of truth in it.

Although Austen was hesitant about revealing herself as an author, she was not hesitant at this point in her life to attempt to publish her writing. Her favorite brother Henry, who lived in London with his wife Eliza, agreed to assist his sister Jane in finding a publisher for her novels. He was much more successful in that endeavor than his father had been. Jane's first published novel, *Sense and Sensibility*, reached print in 1811. It was published anonymously, the title page identifying its author only as "a Lady." The arrangements made with

Thomas Egerton, the publisher, were that the novel would be published at the author's expense (a common practice at the time). Between the sales of the first edition (it completely sold out and another edition was scheduled quickly) and the ownership of copyright, Jane Austen had made 250 pounds from the novel by July 1813. When one considers that the Austen women lived on an income of just over 400 pounds per year, plus a house provided by Edward, one begins to understand the value of such additional income to the Austen women.

After the success of *Sense and Sensibility*, Henry had little difficulty convincing Egerton to publish *Pride and Prejudice*. The publisher bought the novel outright for 110 pounds and published it at his own expense early in 1813. It was published to considerable acclaim and sold out its first edition quickly. In November of 1813, second editions of both *Sense and Sensibility* and *Pride and Prejudice* were published, to be followed quickly by the publication of *Mansfield Park* in May 1814. Jane Austen had finally hit her stride as an author, publishing her works in rapid succession to an excited audience, and continuing to produce works of great merit as the early works received praise from people of all walks of life in England.

Among the admirers of the "Lady" who wrote *Pride and Prejudice* was the Prince Regent of England. When the Prince Regent discovered, through an indiscreet disclosure of Austen's identity by her brother Henry, that the author of *Pride and Prejudice* was in London on a visit, he arranged for his official librarian to begin correspondence with the young author and to invite her to Carlton House, his London home. Through his librarian, the Prince Regent made it clear that he would approve any request that might be made by the author to dedicate her next novel to him. Such an approval was, in fact, essentially an order that such a dedication must be made. The "request" put Austen in a difficult position. She vehemently disapproved of the actions of the Prince Regent, whose lifestyle she considered immoral, yet she felt bound to abide by his wishes because of her respect for the monarchy. The resulting dedication to her next novel, *Emma*, published in 1816, reads as follows: "To His Royal Highness The Prince Regent, this work is, by his Royal Highness's permission, most respectfully dedicated, by His Royal Highness's dutiful and obedient humble servant, The Author." It served her purposes well. Read as a sincere statement of fact, the dedication honors the Prince Regent. Read, however, with a knowledge of her distaste for the Prince Regent as well as the numerous satiric dedications that fill her juvenilia, one recognizes the irony of the dedication. As Brian Wilks indicates in his critical work *Jane Austen*:

The Prince Regent would have no idea that his was merely the last, though perhaps the most distinguished of a long line of satirical dedications. Here the mature Jane Austen was dedicating one of her finest pieces of work to a man whom she disliked, and who represented in his extravagances and indulgences everything that she abhorred and that her novels held up to ridicule. (129)

Regardless of Austen's feelings about the Prince Regent, however, the fact that one of her novels received the imprimatur of the Royal Family as *Emma* did represents an even greater acceptance of her novels by the elite of England and what was essentially a Royal seal upon the novelist's success.

Emma was the last novel Austen published during her lifetime. She continued to write, however, until shortly before her death in 1817. After recovering the manuscript of *Susan* from Messrs. Crosby and Co., she revised it and arranged for its publication as *Northanger Abbey*. She also completed the manuscript of *Persuasion*, which was published, along with *Northanger Abbey*, after her death.

During Jane Austen's last year, perhaps even longer, she suffered from her final illness. In 1965, Sir Zachary Cope, a Fellow of the Royal College of Surgeons, suggested that the symptoms Austen and her family discuss in their last letters were those of Addison's disease. Dr. Eric Beck, consulted by Austen biographer Claire Tomalin for her 1997 *Jane Austen: A Life*, suggests that the symptoms are actually more consistent with a lymphoma such as Hodgkin's disease. Regardless of the specific identity of the disease, the Austen family letters that remain from 1817 indicate the progressive nature of her deterioration. She continued to write when she could but found that her writing could not progress as quickly or as well as previously. She found walking to be difficult and received what little outdoor exercise she could by riding on the back of a donkey.

In May 1817, Austen was moved to Winchester, sixteen miles from Chawton, so that she could receive better medical attention. Her brother James, rector at Steventon since their father's retirement, sent his carriage to transport his sister to a house in College Street. Her brother Henry and nephew William Knight rode alongside the carriage during the journey, a journey conducted almost completely in the rain. Their presence through the difficult journey dramatically demonstrates their devotion to their beloved sister and aunt throughout her life and even in her death.

Jane Austen died peacefully in the arms of Cassandra, on the 18th of July, 1817. Cassandra wrote to Fanny Knight of Jane's death:

till half past four, when she ceased to breathe, she scarcely moved a limb. A slight motion of the head with every breath remaind [sic] till almost the last. I sat close to her with a pillow on my lap to assist in supporting her head, which was almost off the bed, for six hours,—fatigue made me then resign my place to Mrs. J. A. for two hours and a half when I took it again & in about one hour more she breathed her last. I was able to close her eyes myself & it was a great gratification to me to render her these last services. (*Jane Austen's Letters to Her Sister Cassandra* 515)

Cassandra's grief was deep upon losing her sister. She wrote to Fanny shortly after Jane's death: "I have lost a treasure, such a Sister, such a friend as never can have been surpassed.—she was the sun of my life, the gilder of every pleasure, the soother of every sorrow. I had not a thought concealed from her, and it is as if I had lost a part of myself. I loved her only too well, not better than she deserved" (*Jane Austen's Letters to Her Sister Cassandra* 513–514). Such seemed to be the attitude of all who knew the novelist well, that she deserved all the love and respect they could show her.

On July 24, 1817, Jane Austen was buried in Winchester Cathedral, near the middle of the north aisle. A slab of black marble in the pavement marks her grave. It reads:

> In Memory of
> JANE AUSTEN
> youngest daughter of the late
> Revd GEORGE AUSTEN,
> formerly Rector of Steventon in this Country
> she departed this life on the 18th July 1817,
> aged 41, after a long illness supported with
> the patience and the hopes of a Christian.
> The benevolence of her heart,
> the sweetness of her temper, and
> the extraordinary endowments of her mind
> obtained the regard of all who knew her and
> the warmest love of her intimate connections.
> Their grief is in proportion to their affection
> they know their loss to be irreparable,
> but in their deepest affliction they are consoled
> by a firm though humble hope that her charity,
> devotion, faith and purity have rendered
> her soul acceptable in the sight of her
> REDEEMER. (Tomalin 270)

Note that her greatest claim to fame, her writing, is not mentioned on her gravestone. Unlike Shakespeare, Wordsworth, George Eliot, and other famous writers interred at Winchester, Austen's memorial was written to celebrate her as a sister and daughter, not as the shining light of English literature she is recognized to be today.

Following Jane Austen's death, her sister Cassandra took over as executrix of her estate. She burned numerous of her sister's letters and cut portions out of others—all according to Jane's own wishes to maintain privacy in personal matters. She also, with Henry's help, arranged for the publication of Jane Austen's final two books, *Northanger Abbey*, a revision of the earlier *Susan* which Messrs. Crosby and Co. had bought but never published, and *Persuasion*, the final novel completed by Austen before her death. It is due to Cassandra's careful management of the publication of these works, as well as the juvenilia Austen left behind, that we have the works of Austen available that we have today.

2

Literary Heritage

What is probably Jane Austen's most famous statement about her novel writing is the quotation taken from a letter to her nephew in which she refers to her writing as "the little bit (two Inches wide) of Ivory on which I work with so fine a Brush, as produces little effect after much labour" (*Jane Austen: Selected Letters* 189). This quotation has often been used to support the idea that Austen saw her novels as minor stories of little import in a world of finer, more significant writing. Yet nothing could be farther from the truth. The context of this famous quotation is a joke. Her young nephew, Edward, had been writing a novel of his own, but had somehow misplaced two and a half chapters. When Austen heard about the loss in a letter she received, she responded with sympathy and humor. Austen's comment was a way of jokingly distancing herself from the loss, claiming that she could certainly not have stolen the chapters for her own writing since she had not been present to take them, nor would his wildly elaborate, probably gothic, style of writing fit into her own more sedate and detailed form of writing. Her writing style had more in common, she implies, with the popular Dutch miniaturist painters of the time than with the Antiquaries, monastic ruins, and vicious villains of the gothic novel. By comparing her novels with the paintings of the Dutch miniaturists, Austen was, in fact, comparing the subject of her novels with art that was highly honored and appreciated in her day, not belittling it, as is so often assumed by her Victorian and twentieth-century critics and biographers.

Austen believed in the importance of the novel as a literary genre, and she took her own writing as seriously as she did that of the novelists she most respected: Samuel Richardson, Fanny Burney, and Maria Edgeworth. She passionately labored to perfect her novels, and attended closely to the reactions of others to her works. Austen was a voracious reader herself. She knew the place she wanted her novels to take within the tradition of the novel in England, though she seems never to have been confident that they would achieve that level of recognition and importance.

THE BIRTH OF THE NOVEL

The novel had been a recognizable genre of literature in England for less than one hundred years before Austen began writing. Fictional writing had been around for centuries, but the full-fledged novel was a relatively new concept. Daniel DeFoe is often credited as having written the first fully-formed novel in the English language. In *The Life and Strange Surprising Adventures of Robinson Crusoe*, published in 1719, he detailed the exotic experiences of a man isolated from society because of a shipwreck. In the course of the novel, Robinson Crusoe learns how to function on his own in a strange land with the help of a native assistant, local plants and animals, and his own, very British, sense of ingenuity. The first novel in the English language was, thus, an adventure novel. Jonathan Swift, in writing *Gulliver's Travels*, published in 1726, followed DeFoe's lead in producing a fictitious adventure for public consumption. He, however, added the quality of satire to the mix. *Gulliver's Travels* was a broad-sweeping satire of English life and English attitudes that used imagination and fantasy to create its ironic view of the English. The adventure motif used by these two important early novelists continued to influence the development of the novel in England as it evolved into different but related subgenres. Even Jane Austen, in writing novels which have frequently been criticized over the years as being stories in which nothing much really happens, makes use of some of the elements of the adventure novel in her fiction.

THE PICARESQUE

One of the subdivisions of the adventure novel is the picaresque. The picaresque narrative first appeared in Spain in the sixteenth century. It focused on the life of a rogue (which in Spanish is "picaro") and his various escapades, often, though not always, unsavory and/or lascivious in nature. In the original picaresque works, the authors did not attempt to connect the stories into a clear plot with an overarching story line. The story as a whole was less important than its parts. These stories were not, therefore, in any sense novels. As the picaresque evolved over time, however, the picaresque novel developed. In this type of adventure novel, the rogue lives by his wit and his charm as he encounters adventure after adventure. The development of the plot in these novels, while no longer the extremely loose structure of essentially unconnected stories familiar to readers of the original picaresque narrative, rarely becomes as unified as it tends to be in other forms of the novel.

Probably the best known eighteenth-century British novel in the picaresque tradition is Henry Fielding's *Tom Jones*, published in 1749. There is an overarching plot in this novel, one that involves the process of discovering the parentage of a young man while watching him develop from a baby to a (relatively) responsible young man, but the reader rarely focuses on those aspects of the plot. Instead, the reader's attention is drawn to each individual adventure in Tom's life, adventures that do not always contribute in significant and overt ways to the development of the overarching plot of the novel.

Jane Austen's novels do not fall within the tradition of the picaresque. Her novels' plots are very tightly woven with no room for adventures to be thrown into the mix unless they directly advance the plot of the novel as a whole. Nonetheless, she was certainly aware of the picaresque form, as can be seen by some of the stories included in her juvenilia. She was well aware of its importance to the tradition of the English novel, but she chose not to make use of it in her own writing for publication, reserving its use for only a few of her early private and family writings.

THE GOTHIC NOVEL

Another form of the adventure novel that developed in the eighteenth century is the gothic novel. The plots of gothic novels were driven by magic and mystery, the macabre and the weird. The usual plot concerned a young innocent woman whose innocence is threatened by an authority figure (often, though not always, a father, stepfather, uncle, or guardian). Such authorities steal young women away from whatever social structure might be able to assist them, often locking them in castle towers, dungeons or monastic ruins. Horace Walpole is usually considered to be the true creator of the gothic novel in English, with his *Castle of Otranto* (1764) being set in a medieval castle with dark, dank stairways; mysterious rooms; long, dark underground passageways; and trapdoors in the most unexpected of places. The most famous of the gothic writers in Austen's lifetime was Anne Radcliffe, whose five gothic romances were read in almost every literate household in England by the early nineteenth century, including the Austen household. In the traditional gothic novel, a young innocent girl is held captive in a dark and shadowy castle, manor house, or monastery. During that time she undergoes sinister, threatening adventures, not of her own making, which she must survive with her innocence intact. The hero, usually a suitor or relative of the captive woman, must overcome the most horrible of evils in his adventurous pursuit of her in order to win her freedom and, if he is a suitor, bind her innocent self to himself in marriage. If the captive cannot be freed with her innocence intact, she must die. Such is the rule of law in the gothic tradition of adventure literature.

The threats within the gothic novel were largely, and inevitably, of a sexual nature. Guardians of rich orphaned girls would sometimes try to coerce their charges into marriages with themselves or others in order to gain access to the girls' financial resources. Fathers would arrange marriages or clandestine liaisons between their daughters and sadistic, wealthy men, from whom they could then demand money and favors. Rape was often threatened, and sometimes performed, in order to gain cooperation from the captive girls by their captors. Young girls were often drugged as a means of forcing them into "giving up" their "innocence." Some novels, like Matthew Lewis's *The Monk* (1796), even went so far as to include scenes of incest and blasphemy on the part of Church officials.

Jane Austen's novels certainly cannot be termed gothic novels; that category of novel she left to her young nephew Edward to attempt (although he never succeeded in publishing any). But her novels do make use of certain conventions of the gothic novel. Its influence can be seen most clearly in *Northanger Abbey*, which was the revision of her first completed and sold novel *Susan*. In the second volume of *Northanger Abbey*, Austen explores many of the concerns expressed in the gothic novel, but instead of setting the action in a gothic world of darkness, castles, evil counts and priests, handsome heroes, and kidnapped heroines, she places these concerns in a realistic English setting. Austen parodies the trappings of the gothic in this novel, but she does not diminish the importance of the essentially gothic emotional, financial, and physical threat to the heroine.

In *Northanger Abbey*, Catherine Morland, a heroine who, Austen's narrator explains, is completely unlike the typical heroine in a novel, experiences threats to her safety as well as her innocence due to her acquaintance with the Tilney family. That Catherine is not the typical heroine is an extremely important point, just as is the placement of Catherine in determinedly English locale. The threats Catherine faces, essentially the same threats to her innocence as face the gothic heroines, are not safely displaced in this novel by being set in a distant place, time, and way of life; instead they occur right in the heart of England in Austen's present time and in the kinds of settings that young women were encouraged to frequent in real life as well as in the novel. Austen makes fun of the trappings of the gothic novel and of the imaginative flights of fancy

that young girls who read gothic novels often indulged in, but the threats to female innocence and autonomy that are at the heart of the gothic novel are ones
that she takes very seriously in her fiction. *Northanger Abbey* is the novel that
makes that connection most explicitly, but the issue is raised in novel after
novel, making clear the emotional and practical connections between the actual situation of unprotected women in contemporary England and the more
Romantic gothic characters created by writers like Mrs. Radcliffe and Horace
Walpole.

THE EPISTOLARY NOVEL

The adventure novels of the eighteenth century, including the gothic romances, are generally written from the view of an omniscient narrator who
chooses which details to share with the reader and which ones to withhold for
reasons of suspense. Another popular subgenre of the novel where a different
point of view is extremely important is the epistolary novel. The epistolary
novel is structured as a series of letters. All of the letters may be from one particular character to one or more recipients, or they may be written to one set of
characters to another set and back again. The author weaves the story together
by allowing the reader to read the words ostensibly written by the actual character or characters involved in the plot. The result is that the story is told by one
or more characters who participate directly in the activity of the plot. The nar-
ration generally remains close to present time; in other words, the correspon-
dent usually records events shortly after they occur and does not know what the
future consequences of the event or of writing about the event will be. Future
letters detail the consequences of earlier events, along with new events in the
story. Thus the reader learns of events as they happen from the perspective of
the writer or writers of the letters themselves. Each event is, therefore, colored
by the personality and experience of those who write the letters and by the particular moment in which that experience is recorded.

Probably the most famous and respected author of epistolary novels in the
eighteenth century was Samuel Richardson, whose most famous novels include *Pamela, or Virtue Rewarded* (1740), *Clarissa Harlowe* (1747–48), and
The History of Sir Charles Grandison (1753–54), the last of which Austen considered a masterpiece of English writing and her favorite novel of all time. The
eighteenth-century epistolary novel was structured as a series of letters that
were usually written and shared among women. It often explored the subjects
of courtship and romance, as well as whatever other topics the author considered to be of interest to women. Evidence suggests that Austen's earliest versions of both *Sense and Sensibility* and *Pride and Prejudice* were epistolary in
nature. If so, Austen chose to change the narrative point of view at some point

in the revision process and destroyed the earlier versions of the stories. Only one of Austen's adult attempts at writing an epistolary novel presently exists in print. *Lady Susan*, unpublished in Austen's lifetime, survived in fair copy manuscript and was published over fifty years after her death, in 1870, by her nephew, James Edward Austen-Leigh. In it, Lady Susan and her daughter reveal their characters and their intentions clearly in a series of letters addressed to one another as well as to others of their acquaintance. The letters reveal the biting wit and cunning of Lady Susan, in particular. By showing Lady Susan describing her actions and motivations in her own words, Austen creates a character memorable for her charm as well as her ethical misconduct. In *Lady Susan*, Austen demonstrates that her ability to write within the restrictions of the epistolary format is tremendously strong. The fact that she did not see fit to attempt to publish the novel in her lifetime indicates that she probably found it less satisfactory as a work of art than her other completed novels. Its existence, however, together with her juvenile epistolary compositions and her explicit admiration of the talents of novelists of the epistolary tradition such as Richardson and Burney, indicates the importance of the epistolary form to her own vision of herself as a novelist. She did not choose to publish in that mode, apparently understanding its limitations for her artistic vision, but she used it in her composition process and admired the technique when it was used effectively by others.

Although Austen chose to abandon the structure of the epistolary novel at a very early stage in her career, the subject of letters and letter writing continues to be significant in her novels. In *Northanger Abbey*, for example, Austen allows her hero, Henry Tilney, to bring up the subject of letter writing and to comment on the differences between male and female letter writing techniques. While his remarks may be understood simply as the rather condescending comments of an arrogant young man about the habits of journal keeping and letter writing among women, they additionally serve as commentary on the epistolary technique itself. Tilney refuses to believe that a young woman like Catherine Morland does not keep a journal, in part, perhaps, because his expectations of female behavior have been formed by his reading of novels. When Catherine denies keeping a journal, Henry responds:

Perhaps you are not sitting in this room, and I am not sitting by you. These are points in which a doubt is equally possible. Not keep a journal! . . . My dear madam, I am not so ignorant of young ladies' ways as you wish to believe me; it is this delightful habit of journalizing which largely contributes to form the easy style of writing for which ladies are so generally celebrated. Every body allows that the talent of writing agreeable letters is peculiarly female. Nature may have done something, but I am sure it must be essentially assisted by the practice of keeping a journal. (12–13)

The use of a lady's journal as a source for her letter writing is commonplace in the epistolary novel. Fictional heroines incarcerated against their will (like Samuel Richardson's characters Pamela and Clarissa Harlowe) inevitably keep a journal of some kind which they hope to share with parents or the hero at some later date, while heroines writing to friends, sisters, and mothers about the social life they enjoy refer to their journals to glean accurate details about the variety of balls and parties they have attended. In both situations the use of the journal is essential to the formulation of letters in the epistolary novel. When Catherine later expresses her doubts to Henry about "whether ladies do write so much better letters than gentlemen," suggesting her reservations about believing "the superiority was always on our [the female] side," she may be indirectly acknowledging the fact that many letters attributed to female characters in novels are the products of a male author's imagination (13). If, therefore, Henry's expectations of female letter writing ability are based on his reading of fiction, they may be based more on the assumptions and creations of male authors such as Samuel Richardson than they are on Henry's actual experience of women's behavior.

Austen's references to the epistolary novel structure in *Northanger Abbey* are oblique; she never addresses the issue directly. Nonetheless, she does present a judgment on the ways novelists use the epistolary form. When the novels are filled with a "general deficiency of subject, a total inattention to stops, and a very frequent ignorance of grammar," as Henry suggests most women's letters are, they are indeed a subject for ridicule (13). But not all epistolary novels are frivolous and poorly written. In the hands of a master novelist like Fanny Burney or Samuel Richardson, the epistolary novel becomes, according to the novel's narrator, "some work in which the greatest powers of the mind are displayed, in which the most thorough knowledge of human nature, the happiest delineation of its varieties, the liveliest effusions of wit and humour are conveyed to the world in the best chosen language" (22). The epistolary tradition is, therefore, one which earns Austen's respect and admiration.

THE NOVEL OF SENSIBILITY

Samuel Richardson's novels are epistolary in form, but that term describes their structure, not their content. When scholars subdivide the genre of the novel of the eighteenth century in terms of content, Richardson's novels are generally classified as novels of sensibility or sentimental novels. Novels of sensibility, like the twentieth-century psychological novel, explore the inner workings of characters' minds and hearts, particularly of the heroine through whose eyes (and pen, in the case of epistolary novels of sensibility) the story is told. Since eighteenth-century novels of sensibility emphasized feeling over action, most centered on the character of one or more young women of marriageable age and their sentiments about the men pursuing them and their possible futures. Not all ended happily, of course. Richardson's *Clarissa Harlowe* is a prime example of how threatening the world could be for an unprotected young woman in a world filled with predatory men of authority. As in the gothic novels, Richardson's villain holds Clarissa captive, threatens her, and is determined to win her over at any cost. The result is Clarissa's death. But regardless of how the novels of sensibility ended, all provided insight into the author's conception of a young woman's mind and the motivations for her behavior.

Austen's novels are certainly examples of the novel of sensibility, though they are also much more than that classification usually implies. Her first published novel, *Sense and Sensibility*, even uses the word "sensibility" in the title. From Marianne and Elinor Dashwood in *Sense and Sensibility* through Elizabeth Bennet in *Pride and Prejudice*, Fanny Price in *Mansfield Park*, Emma Woodhouse in *Emma*, and Anne Eliot in *Persuasion*, the characters of young women are examined and displayed, both to their advantage and to their disadvantage, creating characters that readers of Austen's time could relate to and understand from their experience of everyday life in England. "Sense," for Austen, was equally as important as "sensibility"; mind and heart must be in harmony in a heroine for her to be the best woman she could be. As a result, Austen's novels depict heroines who are not traditional heroines of the novel of sensibility. They think as well as feel. But without the popularity of the novel of sensibility in England in the eighteenth century, it is unlikely that Austen's depiction of the heart of English women would have been so effective or that she would have found an audience so prepared to read about the inner life of realistic, contemporary women in the novel.

THE WOMEN'S RIGHTS NOVEL

The women's rights novel was a subgenre of the novel that started to gain ground near the end of the eighteenth century, just as Austen was beginning to experiment with writing. The full-blown women's rights novel of the end of the eighteenth century includes characters who are, of course, far afield from Austen's young women of prudence and propriety. Mary Wollstonecraft's novels *Mary* and *Maria, or the Wrongs of Woman* are the best known of this subgenre to twenty-first-century readers. These novels often advocated sexual love outside the bounds of marriage while promoting the idea that marriage is a form of legalized prostitution. They usually insisted that divorce should be a right of women as well as men, based on feelings of incompatibility for either party. The rights of women for custody of their children were addressed, as was the right of a woman to have complete financial autonomy, regardless of marital status. Austen certainly never promoted sexual love outside of marriage, divorce, or a woman's complete autonomy regardless of marriage, but the issue of women's rights and limited autonomy for women is a subject of considerable importance in all of her novels.

Claudia L. Johnson, in her 1988 study *Jane Austen: Women, Politics and the Novel*, discusses the political climate in which Austen wrote. The 1790s, when she composed the first versions of *Northanger Abbey*, as well as *Sense and Sensibility* and *Pride and Prejudice*, was a decade in which the women's rights novel was quite popular as well as controversial. That Austen would choose to enter into the discussion of women's rights raging in England at the time is a logical assumption. Not only were unequivocally radical women novelists such as Mary Wollstonecraft and Mary Hays writing about the unfair subjugation of women, even essentially conservative novelists like Fanny Burney, Maria Edgeworth, Elizabeth Hamilton, and Amelia Opie were advocating change in or, minimally, expressing ambivalence about the status quo and how it affected women. Johnson notes that these latter novelists "smuggle in their social criticism, as well as the mildest of reformist projects, through various means of indirection—irony, antithetical pairing, double plotting, the testing or subverting of overt, typically doctrinaire statement with contrasting dramatic incident" (Johnson xxiii–xxiv). Austen participates in this project as well, and like her contemporaries uses "the device of centering her novels in the consciousness of unempowered characters—that is—women" in order to "expose and explore those aspects of traditional institutions—marriage, primogeniture, patriarchy—which patently do not serve her heroines well" (Johnson xxiv). Austen's novels do "expose and explore" the problems involved in "traditional institutions," especially as they affect the disenfranchised in her society. *Sense and Sensibility* and *Pride and Prejudice* both examine the plight of women who cannot inherit their husbands' estates due to the laws of primogeniture and strict settlement. A careful reading of these novels clearly exposes the dangers such women are subject to, although the characters themselves are saved from dire consequences due to the assistance of distant relatives and acceptable marriages. In the later novels *Emma* and *Persuasion*, the primary characters do not face the possibility of such danger, but the minor characters Mrs. and Miss Bates and Mrs. Smith face not only the possibility; they actually experience poverty and a spiraling down the social ladder upon the death of husbands and fathers. In *Mansfield Park*, the situation of a young girl dependent for her future on her wealthy uncle is explored, as well as the consequences of the law of primogeniture for younger sons who may, in fact, be more worthy of inheriting and managing the family estate than the eldest brothers who, by law and tradition, inherited the bulk of the family property. Through such plots, Austen, like Wollstonecraft and Hays, exposes many of the inequities and injustices of

English social structure at the beginning of the nineteenth century. Her approach is, however, more subtle and indirect than theirs, in part, perhaps, because of the time in which her novels are published.

Although Austen composed the first drafts of at least three novels during the 1790s, when the publication of women's rights novels was at its height, by the eighteen-teens, when Austen published her novels, a tremendous backlash against women's rights and writers of women's rights novels had occurred. Mary Wollstonecraft's openness about the details of her life were held against her, and all writing that we in the twenty-first century would call explicitly feminist was considered to be immoral and virtually unpublishable. The degree of subtlety and indirectness Austen uses in approaching the issue of women's rights is undoubtedly, therefore, in part a result of the decade in which she published. To write more explicitly of society's wrongs against women would have virtually guaranteed that her novels would not have made it into print within her lifetime.

THE DOMESTIC NOVEL

The domestic novel was an extremely popular genre in the eighteenth and nineteenth centuries in England. It, like the novel of sensibility, focused primarily on the lives of women, though it might or might not explore the consciousness of the women involved, as did the novel of sensibility. The essential element of the domestic novel was its setting. It centered, always, in the home, focusing attention on family relationships and the domestic activities of women. It rarely, if ever, addressed issues of business, even family business that went beyond the sales of eggs and dairy products from the wife's small farmyard or the prices of fabric for dresses and drapes. Instead it addressed only those aspects of life considered to be part of the "domestic sphere," that sphere of influence in which women were expected to perform: primarily family nurturance, both physical and spiritual.

Austen's novels certainly include the domestic sphere as an important ingredient. We see women at their sewing, meals being planned and prepared, concern about both the physical and emotional needs of children, neighbors, and friends, and much attention to the issues of courtship and appropriate marriages for the daughters in the family. But none of Austen's novels contain solely domestic issues. Men do engage in business within her pages. For instance, Mr. Knightley discusses farm business with his property manager. Mr. Darcy assists Mr. Bennet and Mr. Gardiner in making a deal with Wickham that will salvage Lydia Bennet's reputation. Captain Wentworth and other naval men and their wives discuss the business of life at sea and make business arrangements involving the spending of the money they have earned at sea. None of these are events that could be central to a traditional domestic novel. Nonetheless, Austen's wide reading would certainly have made her aware of the traditional domestic novel, and she created scenes of domestic employment as vivid and realistic as those of any writer of exclusively domestic fiction.

THE COURTSHIP NOVEL

The courtship novel of eighteenth- and early nineteenth-century England, as defined by Katherine Sobba Green in *The Courtship Novel, 1740–1820: A Feminized Genre*, combines aspects of the domestic novel with aspects of the women's rights novel. It differs from the domestic novel in that it focuses attention on the period of courtship alone, a period of relative autonomy for the young woman between the time of her coming out into society and her marriage. By concentrating attention on this period of the young woman's life, Green suggests that the authors of courtship novels appropriated many of the conventions of the domestic novel for feminist purposes.

Until the middle of the eighteenth century, English fathers and guardians customarily assumed the right to determine their daughters' and female wards' husbands. Young women usually were given the right to refuse to marry someone of their father's choosing who absolutely repulsed them, but they did not have the right to choose their own mates. But even their right of refusal had limits, as their dependence upon father or guardian for survival was often absolute. In the mid-eighteenth century, this practice of paternally-arranged marriages began to give way to the companionate marriage, a marriage in which the marriage partners were expected to choose one another on the basis of affection. The expectation remained that the partners would be of similar economic and social status, and that the marriage would carry familial obligations, but affection and companionship between the marital partners came to be expected, both by the espoused couple and by society at large.

Prior to societal acceptance of the companionate marriage, the period before a young woman's marriage was considered to be a part of her childhood. At marriage her dependence on her father transferred to her husband, giving her no period of life in which her own feelings and desires took priority in her own life or to those to whom she was attached. With the advent of companionate marriage, however, the young woman enjoyed relative autonomy during the time in which she was considered marriageable but was not yet married. She remained financially dependent upon her father or guardian, but in order to find an appropriate mate, she was allowed a degree of freedom to meet and become acquainted with a variety of marriageable men that young women of aristocratic and gentry status in previous generations would not have been allowed. (Among the poor, where there were no fortunes or estates to settle, companionate marriage had been more common, and considerably greater freedom of movement and association had traditionally been allowed.)

The development of the courtship novel coincided with the ideological shift in society from arranged marriage contracts by family authorities to affectionate relationships between two individuals. Marriage itself continued to be treated as a contract between families that had repercussions for all family members, but the choice of a marriage partner became more the responsibility of the individuals involved than it had been before. The courtship novel developed, therefore, to focus on that period of relative autonomy that a young woman of marriageable age had before committing herself to marriage and making herself dependent on a man other than her father or guardian for the remainder of her life. Katherine Sobba Green suggests that what "distinguished courtship novels from their contemporary narratives was that thematically they offered a revisionist view: women, no longer merely unwilling victims, became heroines with significant, though modest, prerogatives of choice and action" (2). Thus, the courtship novel melds aspects of the domestic novel with aspects of the women's rights novel, encouraging women to use what autonomy they were allowed during the period of life in which they were allowed it, while reinforcing the idea that the role of women should inevitably be centered around marriage and the home.

Austen's novels were published during the last years of the time period Green designates as the period of the courtship novel. Her novels, like those Green discusses, focus primarily on the period of her heroines' lives during which they are considered marriageable but are not yet married. They explore young women's range of choices on the marriage market and the reasons for which they choose and refuse various marriage proposals. Austen's heroines often, however, maintain a degree of autonomy within their marriages as well as during their courtship: note Emma Woodhouse remaining in her father's house after her marriage, causing her husband to leave his own home to satisfy her desire to support her father in his home throughout his lifetime. The ideology of companionate marriage allowed women of the landed classes a degree of autonomy not previously available to them. As the courtship novel in general and Austen's novels specifically indicate, by introducing the experience of autonomy into their lives for a short period, it encouraged them to work towards ensuring some degree of autonomy into their lives even as married women.

THE CONDUCT BOOK

The conduct book was a very popular and influential form of literature in eighteenth-century England. Works such as John Gregory's *A Father's Legacy to*

His Daughters (1774) and Lady Sarah Pennington's *An Unfortunate Mother's Advice to Her Absent Daughters* (1761) were written in epistolary format, providing parental advice to young women about how to behave in matters of both the head and the heart. Gregory expressed considerable concern over his daughters' choices of husbands advising that since

> your choice of a husband [is] of the greatest consequence to your happiness, I hope you will make it with the utmost circumspection. Do not give way to a sudden sally of passion, and dignify it with the name of love. Genuine love is not founded in caprice; it is founded in nature, on honourable views, on virtue, on similarity of tastes, and sympathy of souls. (Chapone 186)

Gregory's emphasis throughout his book of advice is on convincing young women to use their heads along with their hearts in choosing life partners and to focus on living respectable lives based on moderation and morality in all things.

Not all conduct books were written in epistolary format. *An Enquiry into the Duties of the Female Sex* (1797), by Thomas Gisborne, for example, was written in the form of a philosophical treatise, as was William Hayley's *A Philosophical, Historical, and Moral Essay on Old Maids* (1785), which advised unmarried women of a certain age to avoid the pitfalls that he considered to be most common for spinsters: too much curiosity, too much affectation in their dress and ornaments, and too much envy and ill nature. These works, among others, presented women of various ages, situations, and classes with voluminous reminders of their duties and obligations in eighteenth-century British society—as formulated by certain British men of a philosophical turn of mind.

Yet another variety of the eighteenth-century British conduct book focused attention on the proper education of children for creating solid British citizens of the aristocracy and gentry. Books such as Hester Chapone's *On the Improvement of the Mind* (1770?), Jane West's *Letters to a Young Lady* (1806), and Catherine Macaulay Graham's *Letters on Education* (1790), advised young women about what kinds of books they should and should not read; what kinds of sewing they should become proficient at; and how important singing, dancing, and playing musical instruments could be to their futures. In addition, these works concentrated on the importance of proper moral conduct and household economy. Chapone combines these characteristics, implying that a woman who does not put the proper emphasis on economy (what in the twentieth century came to be known as "home economics" and "life skills") cannot adequately fulfill her moral duties as a woman in life:

Economy is so important a part of a women's character, so necessary to her own happiness, and so essential to her performing properly the duties of a wife and of a mother, that it ought to have the precedence of all other accomplishments, and take its rank next to the first duties of life. It is, moreover, an art as well as a virtue; and many well-meaning persons, from ignorance, or from inconsideration are strangely deficient in it. (88)

Although Chapone considers the domestic arts of household economy to be one of the highest priorities for a young woman's education, she by no means believes it should be the only area of education. Of the accomplishments a young woman should develop, she writes,

the chief of these is a competent share of reading, well chosen and properly regulated. . . . Dancing, and the knowledge of the French tongue, are now so universal, that they cannot be dispensed with in the education of a gentlewoman; and indeed, they are both useful as well as ornamental: the first by forming and strengthening the body, and improving the carriage; the second, by opening a large field of entertainment and improvement for the mind. . . .

To write a free and legible hand, and to understand common arithmetic, are indispensable requisites.

As to music and drawing, I would only wish you to follow as genious [innate ability] leads. (109–111)

Chapone's educational advice includes advice on what to read as well as what to avoid. It, like the majority of such educational treatises of the day, concentrates on proper education for *women*, assuming, it seems, that the traditional classical education was best suited for developing proper British gentlemen.

The conduct books so popular in the eighteenth century make their appearance in Austen's novels primarily through the person of Mr. Collins in *Pride and Prejudice*. There, Mr. Collins, a clergyman with a talent for being both boring and obsequious, decides to read to the Bennet girls from *Sermons for Young Women* (1766) by the Rev. James Fordyce. Austen does not refer to any specifics from Fordyce's sermons, but she makes it clear from the reactions of Mr. Collins's listeners (as well as from the fact that it is Mr. Collins who chooses the reading) that such sanctimonious books of advice from those who know nothing of what it is to be a young woman are not the most effective way of advising and educating young women. Conduct books of the period are a very good source of information about contemporary expectations of behavior from the young women of the time, but they may not, Austen implies, always have been the most effective way of eliciting that behavior from the young women themselves.

CONCLUSION

Although her formal education was minimal, Jane Austen was extremely well-read in the literature of her day. She had free run of her father's library during her youth and young adulthood, and that library was extensive, undoubtedly containing the classics of ancient Greece and Rome, contemporary histories and works of political importance, as well as the major masterpieces of British poetry, prose, and drama. From her letters, novels, and other writings, it is clear that Jane Austen's reading choices were both varied and abundant. Her letters mention her reading and seeing performances of many of the popular dramas of the day. She writes about reading various popular histories; travel literature, such as John Carre's *Travels in Spain*; political works such as *Essay on the Military Police and Institutions of the British Empires*; the poetry of Cowper (her favorite), Byron, and others; French novels by Madame de Genlis; and English novels by authors as varied as Samuel Richardson, Sir Walter Scott, Maria Edgeworth, Charlotte Lennox, Sydney Owenson, Hannah More, Mary Brunton, and Fanny Burney.

Austen's letters reflect her wide-ranging interests in literature. But even more important, her novels reflect those interests, in her attention to the smallest detail in everything from the ships' names and descriptions she used in *Persuasion* to the title of the proper conduct book that a man with Mr. Collins's particular personality would choose to read to his young unmarried cousins and the particular plays that the Bertrams would consider presenting in *Mansfield Park*. Each of these details relay significant information about the characters in Austen's novels for readers of her time, who would have understood her references to particular works of literature just as readers of today would understand references to Stephen King or *Star Wars*. But in addition to references to well-known works of literature and historical detail, she also used the various forms of literature themselves, molding and shaping them to satisfy the needs of her own fiction rather than allowing herself to fall into writing in any one particular traditional form. Austen was clearly an author who wrote within the tradition in which she was born and educated, but she did more than that. She used the traditional forms to expand the novel. If Austen can be said to write within any particular tradition, it is the tradition of the greatest of novels, a tradition she herself defined as "some work in which the greatest powers of the mind are displayed, in which the most thorough knowledge of human nature, the happiest delineation of its varieties, the liveliest effusions of wit and humour are conveyed to the world in the best chosen language" (22).

3

Sense and Sensibility
(1811)

The first novel published by Jane Austen was *Sense and Sensibility*, a story which focuses on a mother and her three daughters who are forced to rely on the kindness of distant relations and friends for support when those nearest in blood and obligation refuse to fulfill their duties. It is also a love story. The two older daughters are in love and considering marriage during much of the novel.

Sense and Sensibility began its existence as *Elinor and Marianne*, a story written in the 1790s while Jane Austen lived at her father's rectory in Steventon. While no copy of the original manuscript is available to examine today, it is clear from Austen's letters and the writings of other members of her family that the form that *Elinor and Marianne* took was that of the epistolary novel, a novel written as though it were a series of letters between close friends and family members.

Over time, Austen decided to revise the novel extensively, changing it from the epistolary format to one that used an outside narrator. The completed novel *Sense and Sensibility* is, therefore, written in the third-person point of view, though presenting the story primarily from the perspective of the eldest Dashwood daughter, Elinor.

The time that passed between the writing of *Elinor and Marianne* and its revision into *Sense and Sensibility* probably resulted in a more sophisticated handling of the subject of the difficulties faced by women whose male provider had died. When Austen wrote the first version of the novel, she was living in the comfort and security of her childhood home, her father's rectory in Steventon.

In the intervening years, however, her father retired from his position as rector, which forced the family to leave their home. Rev. and Mrs. Austen, together with their daughters, Cassandra and Jane, moved to lodgings in Bath, a resort town in England. While in Bath, Austen's father died, leaving his wife and daughters with very little income of their own, dependent on the kindness of the Austen sons and other friends.

After spending considerable time attempting to find decent, affordable lodgings in Bath, the Austen women left the resort town and spent the next two and a half to three years staying in lodgings elsewhere and "visiting," staying for relatively lengthy periods with a succession of family members and friends. During this period they had no place to call their own. Finally, in 1809, they moved into Chawton Cottage, a home provided for them by one of Jane's brothers, Edward. It was at Chawton Cottage that Jane completed her revisions of *Sense and Sensibility,* and from Chawton Cottage that she, with the help of her brother Henry, published this first novel anonymously. Undoubtedly the experience of living in a household with no male provider during those years affected the revision of the novel from *Elinor and Marianne* to *Sense and Sensibility.* A novel in which sisters are forced from their childhood home in reduced circumstances to find other shelter and friends to care for them resonates deeply with Austen's own life during those years.

PLOT DEVELOPMENT

The plot of *Sense and Sensibility* develops primarily through a series of promises, both spoken and implied, between the male characters in the story and the women of the Dashwood and Steele families. These women, having no responsible men to take care of them nor sufficient financial assets with which to take care of themselves are especially dependent on the promises of men and particularly susceptible to difficulties due to the broken promises of the men around them. As the novel opens, we are told that the "family of Dashwood had long been settled in Sussex," and that the old gentleman who owned Norland Park intended to "bequeath" the estate to his nephew and his family, who came to live with him and provided him with comfort, assistance, and enjoyment in his final years (1). Such an inheritance would allow Mr. Dashwood to provide well for all of his family, a son who had been born of his first marriage, and three daughters born to him in his second.

The estate is, indeed, left to Mr. Dashwood upon his uncle's death, but a condition on the inheritance makes it impossible for him to assure his wife and daughters' security as he desires. His uncle leaves the estate to him with the condition that it be passed on in its entirety to his son, John Dashwood, upon his death. Such provisions in wills were very common at that period in history;

nonetheless, it presents Mr. Dashwood with a dilemma. His son is already well provided for by money left to him by his late mother, the first Mrs. Dashwood. The second Mrs. Dashwood and her three daughters, however, will have almost no support after Mr. Dashwood's death. Under the circumstances, all that Mr. Dashwood can do is to extract a promise from his son that he will take care of his stepmother and sisters in the future. John Dashwood promises to do so, but the details of what might constitute such caretaking are not specified between the two men. Mr. Dashwood then dies, leaving John in charge of the estate and responsible for the welfare of the rest of his family.

As the novel continues, John Dashwood and his wife Fanny, take over the estate immediately after Mr. Dashwood's death, leaving Mrs. Dashwood and her daughters to feel like unwanted visitors in the home that Mrs. Dashwood had been mistress of when her husband was alive. Because they are so clearly unwanted at Norland Park, Mrs. Dashwood decides that she must remove herself and her daughters from the situation they find themselves in. Finally she is offered a cottage, at very low rent, from a distant cousin in Devonshire. Their new home is quite distant from their old neighborhood. Since John has yet to fulfill the promise his stepmother knows he made to his father, she expects him to do so at the time of the move, but he offers Mrs. Dashwood and his sisters absolutely nothing, not even assistance in moving their belongings to their new residence. Thus, with no help from the wealthy man of the family, the Dashwood women move to Devonshire where they become the tenants of Sir John Middleton, a distant cousin and reliable friend. There, with the assistance of the Middletons (who make a point of fulfilling any promises they make), they create a relatively secure home for themselves.

The plot continues to develop through a series of both actual and implied promises by men who are romantically interested in the two oldest Dashwood daughters. While still at Norland Park, Elinor learns to care for Edward Ferrars, the brother of her sister-in-law, Fanny Dashwood. Although Edward never verbally suggests a future commitment to Elinor, his behavior towards her is interpreted by Elinor, her family, and her friends as that of a suitor. His sister Fanny and their mother, both of whom intend that Edward marry a woman of wealth and position, discourage the relationship. But the Dashwood women, analyzing Edward's behavior towards Elinor, assume that he has the intention of pursuing a marital commitment with her when he obtains the financial ability to do so. The fact that Mrs. Ferrars, Edward's mother, controls the financial affairs in their family (an unusual though not unheard of situation in Austen's time) creates a serious financial impediment to Edward's marrying according to his own wishes at this point in his life.

Mrs. Ferrars's ambitions for her son are not, however, the only thing holding him back from openly promising to marry Elinor. Instead, as we discover later in the novel, Edward has already made such a promise to another young woman, Lucy Steele, the niece of the tutor with whom he lived as a boy. Edward, having promised Lucy that they would marry at the appropriate time, feels obligated to fulfill that promise—even though he made the promise when he was a foolish young boy and the person he truly loves is Elinor. With Elinor, therefore, he avoids making any overt promises of marriage or a future together, though he clearly understands that, by engaging her affections as he does, he is leading her to believe that they will have a future together. Such a mixture of spoken and unspoken promises creates difficulties for both young women. Lucy Steele, upon hearing rumors of the assumed engagement of Elinor and Edward, plots to retrieve her primacy in the life of the man she plans to marry. She callously and calculatedly confides her secret engagement in Elinor, relying on Elinor's sense of integrity and honor to force her to back away from Edward (109). She also attempts to ingratiate herself into the lives of Edward's family and friends in order to convince them of her superiority, assuming that, by that means, she will make herself into someone who will be considered by his family to be good enough for marriage to him when news of the secret engagement comes out.

Lucy's machinations backfire. When Edward's mother discovers that he has been secretly engaged for years to the orphaned and dependent niece of his tutor, she disowns her eldest son and immediately bestows the inheritance expected by the eldest on her younger son, Robert, leaving Edward to fend for himself. Lucy, however, being more interested in marrying into the Ferrars fortune than she ever was in marrying Edward for the sake of himself, transfers her affections to the younger son, who at that point has complete control of the Ferrars fortune. She hurries him into a quick elopement. The result is that Edward is poor but free to approach Elinor openly.

Once his mother has disinherited him, Edward decides to make his own way in a profession of his own choice. He enters training to become a clergyman, hoping eventually to have a church of his own. Elinor's good friend, Colonel Brandon, himself having been thwarted from marrying the woman he loved by family politics, provides Edward with the job of rector of a church in his own community, thus providing him with a home and income on which he is able to marry Elinor. Thus, one might think, all is well that ends well, but an examination of the situation shows just how tenuous the situation had been, and in how much danger Edward's verbalized and implied promises left both Lucy and Elinor.

Lucy Steele, as a young woman with no father or mother and no income of any kind, is completely dependent on friends and family to support her. She spends most of her life as a single young woman visiting in the homes of one or another friend or relative. Her behavior, therefore, has to be ingratiating in every situation so that she will continue to be welcome in those homes. Without an income of her own and with no influential connections, her determination to remain among the gentry rather than to sink into the servant or highly impoverished spinster class can only be fulfilled through her deliberate manipulations of those around her. If Edward had publicly rejected her after it was known that she had been secretly engaged to him *before* she had achieved marriage to another man of means, her reputation would have been seriously tarnished, and most of the friendships she relies upon for support would be withdrawn, leaving her destitute and dishonored.

Edward's unspoken promise to Elinor is likewise problematic. Although he never spoke to her of a marriage between them prior to Lucy's marriage to his brother, his behavior encouraged Elinor to believe that he was in love with her and would want to spend his life with her. The one primary stumbling block, as she saw it, was the attitude of his mother, Mrs. Ferrars, who wanted Edward to marry a woman of wealth and position, not the dependent sister-in-law of her daughter Fanny. Elinor's assumption was, of course, only partially correct. Certainly Mrs. Ferrars's refusal to provide Edward with his inheritance made it difficult for him to marry without a profession, but his earlier promise to Lucy also stood in the way of a commitment. Nonetheless his behavior towards Elinor encouraged her and her friends and family to consider them, for all practical purposes, to be betrothed. Thus Elinor, whose financial circumstances, like Lucy's, required that she find a mate who could provide for her, found herself attached emotionally to a young man who was, ethically and practically, unavailable to marry her. Despite that fact that Austen manipulates the plot in such a way as to allow Edward and Elinor to marry and be comfortably provided for in the end, the story demonstrates the dangers to which women of little means are subject when they must rely exclusively on men's promises, verbalized and implied, for their support.

Elinor's sister Marianne also faces considerable danger due to the faithlessness of men. In fact, her experience almost costs her life. Upon moving to Devonshire, Marianne meets a handsome young rogue by the name of Willoughby who behaves very romantically but with great impropriety towards her. Although Willoughby never verbally promises Marianne any commitment for the future, he treats her as though they are betrothed from very early in the relationship. Willoughby, like Edward, is dependent upon a relative for his future wealth, although he, unlike Edward, has a small fortune of his own even without inheriting his aunt's estate. Willoughby knowingly and intentionally toys with Marianne's emotions at the beginning of their acquaintance. Later in the story, he admits that he did, in fact, come to care about her deeply and to regret the pain that he had caused her when he felt forced to snub her in London society. He also admits, however, that he never intended to marry her, regardless of

STUDENT COMPANION TO JANE AUSTEN

how he had behaved towards her. Knowing himself and his requirements of life, he always knew that he must marry a woman of wealth who could provide him with greater fortune than would otherwise attach itself to him. The woman he married must also be one whom his relations would approve and reward him for marrying. Marianne, as a dependent woman with almost no income of her own, would not, he was certain, be acceptable to his family connections (267–275).

Marianne's reputation was seriously compromised. Many of the activities she and Willoughby engaged in—riding alone through the countryside, taking long walks alone together, writing letters when apart from each other—were considered to be appropriate only for an engaged couple, and some were pushing the limits of propriety even for the betrothed. They were completely inappropriate for unmarried men and women of less formal commitment. Such behavior on Marianne's part could easily have caused her to be labeled an easy woman, disreputable and unmarriageable. Fortunately, Austen includes in her story Colonel Brandon, a man of considerable income and position who has had personal experience with the character of Willoughby, experience that enables him to recognize just how conniving and despicable Willoughby can be to young women who are not adequately protected.

Colonel Brandon had been disappointed in love when he was a very young man by the connivances of his father and brother, who forced the young woman he was in love with into a very unhappy and abusive marriage with his brother. She eventually left her husband's home and fell into a dishonorable and disreputable life, dying young and leaving an illegitimate daughter, whom Brandon then took and supported. This daughter, Eliza (named for her mother), when a teenager, was seduced by Willoughby and left alone and pregnant. Brandon, knowing Willoughby's reputation as well as his behavior with the young Eliza, is much less judgmental of Marianne for her overly free behavior with Willoughby than others might be. He also maintains a degree of vigilance over her and her family, attempting to prevent the same kind of disaster from happening to Marianne that has befallen his young ward.

In the end, after Marianne suffers a life-threatening disease, in large part as a result of her disappointment over Willoughby's betrayal of her, Colonel Brandon wins her heart and provides her with a wonderful home as her husband. His promises, both spoken and unspoken, to take care of her and her family are fulfilled to the fullest extent. His constancy and commitment are the strongest of any man's in the novel.

Each twist and turn throughout the plot of *Sense and Sensibility* hinges on a promise, spoken or implied, made or broken. From John Dashwood's promise at his father's deathbed, a promise broken, through Colonel Brandon's promise to support his wife and her family for the rest of their lives, a promise kept, promises dictate the movement of the narrative in this, Austen's first published novel.

CHARACTER DEVELOPMENT

Most of the characters in *Sense and Sensibility* are developed as sets of pairs, each character being developed individually, but also as a character more fully understood and explored by comparison and contrast with another character within the story. Just as the title links the terms "sense" and "sensibility," so does the story link the characters of Elinor and Marianne, John Dashwood and Sir John Middleton, Edward and Robert Ferrars, and Willoughby and Colonel Brandon into contrasting pairs that can best be understood when examined in terms of each other.

Elinor and Marianne are the primary pairing of the novel. They are the two young women at the heart of the novel, and are usually designated as the representatives of "Sense" and "Sensibility" respectively. Elinor is seen as the sensible one. She is the one Mrs. Dashwood seeks out to counsel her on the most appropriate behavior upon leaving Norland Park (4). She admires "sense and goodness" above all things (16), even in the man she hopes to marry. She is much more conscious of the costs of things (both financial and social) than either her mother or Marianne and encourages decisions based upon consideration of logical conclusions. Elinor also demonstrates more sense about love than her sister. Despite very deep feelings for Edward Ferrars, Elinor does not step beyond the bounds of propriety in her actions towards him. Nor does she *assume* his intentions; despite the views of those around her, Elinor refuses to trust that Edward has plans of marrying her until he actually proposes.

Marianne, on the other hand, is a romantic at heart. Sensibility is, perhaps, her strongest characteristic. Her emotions run high and strong. When she hears Edward read from the poet Cowper with less than intense emotion, she is horrified. She wonders how her sister can abide such a man. But, she acknowledges, "Elinor has not my feelings, and therefore she may overlook it, and be happy with him" (14). Marianne relishes the wildness of nature and extremes of emotion. She falls in love with Willoughby, in large part, because of his intensity and his refusal to adhere to propriety when such adherence goes against his inclinations. At the outset of the novel, Marianne considers "sensible" men like Colonel Brandon to be dull and suited for marriage only with some old spinster who does not mind trading her nursing and caretaking skills for a good house and income (31–32). Such men, she tells her sister, could not possibly arouse passion in any person who has any degree of sensibility.

In the course of the novel, Austen indicates that adhering solely to either characteristic, sense or sensibility, is problematic. Elinor's insistence on behaving sensibly leads her to suffer great emotional turmoil over her feelings towards Edward. The fact that she does not reveal, even to her mother and sister, the heartache she feels when Lucy tells her of her engagement to Edward demonstrates her high moral character and determination always to behave with propriety, but it also deprives her of the emotional support she desperately needs at that time. Additionally it allows Edward to tell himself that he has not seriously injured her through his own dishonorable behavior, something that the reader knows very well is untrue. Some mixture of sensibility with her sense might have allowed Elinor to find support for her state of mind as well as to encourage Edward and Lucy into being somewhat more responsible for their actions than they were otherwise. Sense alone, therefore, does not produce the most well-rounded of heroines in Austen's work.

Sensibility alone, however, is an even bigger problem. Marianne's determination to act on her feelings at all times, to engage in activities considered by most to be indecorous, if not downright immoral, causes discomfort and even great distress to many among her family and friends. Elinor, for instance, is frequently forced to lie for her in order to maintain politeness and propriety when Marianne does not feel the desire for company. And on a more serious note, Marianne's determination to indulge the extremes of emotion, combined with her love of walking in the wildnesses of nature, eventually leads to her near-fatal illness (257). After recovering from that illness, however, Marianne comes to understand the need to moderate her sensibility with some degree of sense. She decides to study more and to become calmer and more discerning. In time she even comes to love Colonel Brandon, the man she had earlier in the novel referred to as a man "old enough to be *my* father" and one who "must have long outlived any sensation" like love (31). By the end of the novel both Elinor and Marianne operate through a combination of sense and sensibility—with sense as the predominant characteristic, but certainly not the only one.

Another pairing of characters that reveals great contrasts in behavior in the novel is that of John Dashwood and Sir John Middleton. Both of these men are heads of households, and as such, they are ethically (though not always legally) responsible for the individuals dependent upon those households. John Dashwood, as the son of Henry Dashwood and heir to Norland Park, has an ethical obligation by the standards of his society to provide for his stepmother and sisters after his father's death. And, just in case the reader doesn't consider the societal obligation already in place to be sufficient motivation, Austen increases the obligation significantly by having Henry Dashwood, on his deathbed, ask for and receive John's explicit promise that he would, indeed, take care of the future needs of his stepmother and sisters (3). The fact that John allows Fanny to talk him out of fulfilling his obligations to his family demonstrates his weakness of character as well as his selfishness. He *knows* the difference between right and wrong, but he allows that knowledge to be rationalized away. His desire to hold on to everything he considers his, even when doing so is likely to leave his own sisters with inadequate support, demonstrates just how little family loyalty and true compassion exist in John Dashwood's heart.

Sir John Middleton, by taking in relatives so distant to him that no one would expect him to feel an obligation to them, demonstrates the kind of selflessness and compassion that a proper head of a family should display. He not only provides them with a place to live that they can both afford and be comfortable in; he also offers them "every accommodation from his own house and garden," including the use of his carriage; almost daily invitations to dinner; gifts of vegetables, fruit and game from his estate; the sharing of his newspaper; and even mailing and collecting their letters for them (no small favor since in Austen's time payment for letters was made on receipt and could be quite expensive) (24–25). Such services traditionally fall to the head of the household, but upon John Dashwood's abdication of his duties towards his family in that role, the more distant relative Sir John Middleton takes them on.

Sir John is in many ways a silly and shallow man whose focus is often on hunting and his hunting buddies. He is no great intellectual and, as a young man, chose a wife of even less intelligence and wit than himself. But he is a man who understands duty to family and is both kind and openhearted. He supplies the needs of the Dashwood women joyfully and with "real satisfaction," their "comfort [being] an object of real solicitude to him" (25). The contrast between Sir John Middleton and John Dashwood, therefore, enables the reader to appreciate the former much more fully and to make the latter appear even more hard-hearted and selfish than he might otherwise seem for his treatment of the dependent women in his family.

Edward and Robert Ferrars are brothers whose differences expose the fashionable prejudices of many people of the time. Edward Ferrars is the eldest son of a wealthy man who died leaving the division of his estate to his widow's discretion. As the eldest son, Edward expects and is expected to inherit the primary estate, leaving his brother Robert the usual smaller inheritance of a younger son. Edward is educated privately at the home of Mr. Pratt, a respectable tutor with whom Edward lived for most of his adolescence. The narrator describes Edward's basic character following his schooling as "too diffident to do justice to himself," but asserts that "when his natural shyness was overcome, his behaviour gave every indication of an open affectionate heart" (12). In addition, his "understanding was good, and his education had given it solid improvement" (12). A young man who displays "an open affectionate heart" combined with "good" understanding improved by education would seem to be the ideal young man to handle an estate benevolently and responsibly, but his mother and sister (John Dashwood's wife, Fanny) doubt his suitability to become the head of their family. They expect the heir of the family to engage in a significantly more elaborate lifestyle than Edward wants to lead. Austen's narrator tells us that

he was neither fitted by abilities or disposition to answer the wishes of his mother and sister, who longed to see him distinguished. . . . They wanted him to make a fine figure in the world. . . . His mother wished to interest him in political concerns, to get him into parliament, or to see him connected with some of the great men of the day. [His sister] wished it likewise; but in the mean while, till one of these superior blessings could be attained, it would have quieted her ambition to see him driving a barouche. But Edward had no turn for great men or barouches. (12)

Edward is not a fashionable young man. He does not display great sensibility, which Marianne considers to be one of his great failings. In fact, if he did, he would undoubtedly impress his mother and sister more favorably. He sees himself as "an idle, helpless being" since his dependence upon inheriting the family estate and fortune has encouraged him never to develop any real motivation to make something useful of himself (88). His primary belief is in the importance of fulfilling one's duty. This belief results in his resolution to marry Lucy Steele even after he has outgrown his youthful fascination for her and despite his family's determination to disown him if he does not give her up. Upon losing the fortune he has expected to inherit, he chooses to enter the profession of clergyman, where he intends to serve his parishioners well, fulfilling his duty to God and the community in which he serves. Yet he does not always, especially in his youth, behave with the utmost of propriety—note his leading Elinor to believe they might have a future together when he is already engaged to Lucy.

Robert Ferrars, on the other hand, is very much the fashionable young man. The first time that the reader sees him in the novel is in a jeweler's shop, selecting an ivory toothpick case for himself. Elinor, waiting for the clerk, examines the young man closely. What she saw was "a person and face, of strong, natural, sterling insignificance, though adorned in the first style of fashion" (186). Elinor's perception is supported by the narrator's observations of Robert's behavior:

At last the affair was decided. The ivory, the gold, and the pearls, all received their appointment, and the gentleman having named the last day on which his existence could be continued without the possession of the toothpick-case, drew on his gloves with leisurely care, and bestowing another glance on the Miss Dashwoods, but such a one as seemed rather to demand than express admiration, walked off with an happy air of real conceit and affected indifference. (186)

This first view of Robert solidly sets up the dramatic contrast between the Ferrars brothers that eventually develops into the disinheritance of the elder in favor of the younger. Earlier in the novel when the reader is told how much Edward's lack of fashion and fitness to be a great man disturbs his mother and sister, the narrator comments ironically that "[f]ortunately he had a younger brother who was more promising" (12). The promise that Robert Ferrars displays is that of a conceited young man who wants to make a fine and fashionable figure, but who cares very little about anything else. His elaborate decision-making process over the choice of decoration on a toothpick case is the most thought that Austen ever shows him putting into anything in the course of the novel. His advancement over his brother to the position of heir to the family estate seems to cause him no twinge of conscience, and his choice of a marriage partner seems to be based more on spontaneous whim and a desire to usurp his brother in matters of the heart than on conscious and conscientious thought. In all things, Robert thinks only of himself and his own desires. He has no sense of duty or obligation to anything else. In this selfish behavior he is continually reinforced by his mother and sister (as well as much of the society of which they are a part) who continue to reward him for his adherence to their own superficial standards even after he has made a financially and socially foolish marriage.

The contrast between the brothers continues to the very end of the book. Robert, the fashionable, selfish son, receives the estate and the support of his family—even though he actually marries, without his family's permission, the very woman Edward was disinherited for having become secretly engaged to. The direct opposition of the brothers at this point in the story enables the reader to understand more clearly the unfairness of Mrs. Ferrars's behavior towards her sons. It also demonstrates the reality that those who are most cognizant of and devoted to duty are not necessarily best rewarded by society, though, as Austen clarifies, Edward "might be supposed no less contented with his lot, no less free from every wish of exchange" with his brother despite his mother's unfair treatment (320).

Yet another important contrasting pair of characters in *Sense and Sensibility* is Colonel Brandon and Willoughby. Both are attracted to Marianne from the moment they meet her, and both are linked (though in different ways) with Eliza Williams. Marianne could, however, have no two more different suitors. Willoughby represents the characteristic of sensibility at its most destructive and disreputable. Colonel Brandon, by contrast, demonstrates the ultimate in sensible and respectable love.

The behaviors of Brandon and Willoughby to the two young Elizas could not have been more different. Brandon truly and deeply loved his Eliza, wanted to marry her, and yet gave up all possibility of being with her (even of seeing her) once she became the wife of his brother in order to protect her reputation and allow her time to attempt to make a satisfying life with his brother. Such was Brandon's sensible and considerate response to an extremely difficult situation. Willoughly, on the other hand, merely used the younger Eliza, a teenage girl infatuated with the older, more sophisticated and fashionable man. He had no honorable intentions towards her and left her alone, friendless, and pregnant. His interest was only in satisfying his own desires, allowing his feelings to hold sway, regardless of the consequences. These, then, are the suitors that Marianne Dashwood has to choose from: a sensible, duty-bound, caretaking gentleman and a callous young rogue who follows the urgings only of his feelings of the moment. Marianne does not, of course, know the histories of her suitors until late in the novel, but their behavior towards her and her family might have given her hints in the right direction were she less attracted to the extremes of sensibility and more willing to recognize the real feelings of a sensible man. While Willoughby whisks her off, at a moment's notice, on treks around the countryside, even taking her into the home of his aunt and showing her around as though they were an engaged couple with permission to view the home (neither of which was true), Brandon quietly watches and waits for opportunities to be of true service to the young woman he is growing to love, as well as to her family. He, unlike Willoughby, makes no great show of his affection. Instead he assists Elinor by giving Edward the position of rector at his community's church; he travels personally to get Mrs. Dashwood when Marianne is deathly ill; and he assists the women in a number of other quiet, almost unnoticeable ways that make their lives easier. His constancy and consideration do much to win Marianne's heart. On the heels of such callous and calculated behavior as Willoughby's, Colonel Brandon, though lacking in the extremes of sensibility in which Willoughby excels, comes to appeal very much to Marianne's post-illness inclinations. Austen's narrator assures us that "Marianne could never love by halves; and her whole heart became, in time, as much devoted to her husband, as it had once been to Willoughby" (321). Only through contrast with a sensibility-filled rogue such as Willoughby would a sensible, self-effacing man like Colonel Brandon be able to win the heart of Marianne Dashwood.

THEMATIC ISSUES

The focus on duty and propriety, or the lack thereof, that concerns each character in *Sense and Sensibility* is the dominant theme of the novel. Edward Ferrars demonstrates perhaps the most overt attempt to follow duty rather than inclination. Upon being disinherited by his mother for refusing to break his engagement to Lucy despite the fact that he no longer has any desire to marry her, he approaches Lucy and gives her the option of breaking the engagement herself. "I thought it my duty," he told Elinor, "independent of my feelings, to give her the option of continuing the engagement or not, when I was renounced by my mother, and stood to all appearance without a friend in the world to assist me" (310–311). Duty, therefore, both motivates him to give Lucy the option of continuing or breaking the engagement and, upon her choosing to continue the engagement, keeps him obligated to marry her despite his changed feelings.

Duty to family is also a concern of Colonel Brandon, as he does his utmost to care for his dying sister-in-law after he discovers the horrible situation into which his cruel brother has forced her. He also provides for his sister-in-law's infant daughter, despite the talk that surrounds her birth and his taking her in. Never does he defend himself against accusations that the child is his own illegitimate daughter; instead he does what he considers to be his duty to her while caring very little, if at all, about what others think of him. His knowledge that he is doing what is right sustains him.

Men like John Dashwood and Willoughby, by contrast, avoid their duty to family and friends, following instead the dictates of their own desires. Although Fanny Dashwood is instrumental in convincing her husband not to provide any assistance to his stepmother and sisters despite his promise to his father, it is John's decision to abdicate that responsibility. Fanny can coerce and convince, but only John has the power to actually grant or withhold the provisions to which he is morally obligated. Willoughby, likewise, knows the duty he owes his aunt not to use her home in inappropriate ways, yet he insists on taking Marianne there for a tour as though she is assured of being the next mistress of the manor when he knows full well that she is not. He knows that his seduction of young Eliza Williams is wrong and that he is duty-bound to care for such a girl once she has succumbed to him. Yet he abandons her, pregnant. He is aware that his behavior is raising expectations of marriage in Marianne while knowing absolutely that he has no intention of marrying a woman without substantial wealth of her own. In Austen's creations of these selfish and self-absorbed characters, she demonstrates the importance of an adherence to duty in her society as well as the dangers that arise from an avoidance of it, not only for those who do the avoiding, but often even more fully for those dependent upon them.

While the fulfillment and/or avoidance of duty is primarily the concern of men in the novel, the issue of propriety is predominantly the realm of the women. When Marianne begins to receive visits from Willoughby, Elinor, who is always extremely careful to behave with the utmost propriety herself, indicates that she wishes the "attachment" between her sister and her apparent suitor were less openly demonstrated, and even "once or twice did venture to suggest the propriety of some self-command" to Marianne (44). Marianne, however, believes that any concealment of emotion is dishonest and is unwilling, as a result, to concern herself in the least with propriety. Her disregard for propriety ends up endangering her reputation and, ultimately, even her life.

To at least one woman in the novel, the *appearance* of propriety is more important than propriety itself. To almost everyone around her, Lucy Steele presents an impenetrable façade of propriety. Only Edward and Elinor are aware that she has, in fact, allowed herself to be secretly engaged to a young man who was not even of age at the time they committed themselves to each other. Such behavior was, at that time in history, extraordinarily improper. And yet, Lucy, in order to try to guarantee marriage within the gentry class, indulges herself in it. In public, however, she appears to be as pure, honorable, and helpful as any proper young woman could be. When the Steele sisters arrive at Sir John Middleton's home for a visit, Lucy immediately becomes the favorite of almost everyone in the household. She praises the children, which wins over Lady Middleton, and makes herself indispensable as someone ready at all times to fulfill any need from babysitting to mending to simply keeping company with those wealthier and more powerful than herself (100–103). Lucy understands that the appearance of propriety, even if it requires direct lies as well as omissions of truth, is essential if she is to make a marriage that will enable her to rise in the world. Unlike Marianne, whose actual behavior is much less offensive than Lucy's but whose refusal to conceal or tone down her feelings places her in a position that threatens her reputation and her life, Lucy calculates and manipulates her way into a profitable marriage with a fashionable young man who, like her, has no qualms about getting what he wants, when he wants it, no matter who gets hurt in the process.

Marrying a man with sufficient income to support them well was essential to women of the gentry and aristocracy in Austen's England. In order to do so, their reputations generally had to be beyond reproach. Therefore, attention to propriety was important to all women, but most especially to those, like the Dashwood and Steele sisters, who had no wealth of their own to make them attractive mates. Even the slightest appearance of impropriety could damage such a woman for life. In *Sense and Sensibility*, Austen demonstrates those dangers, while also showing that a woman can, on occasion, get a second chance.

A FEMINIST READING OF *SENSE AND SENSIBILITY*

Literature written by and about women lends itself very well to feminist interpretative approaches of various kinds. Such approaches often examine the literature of earlier centuries for signs of discontent with or subversive suggestions against aspects of a society in which men have exclusive control of power.

Such an approach is especially fruitful to use when examining Jane Austen's novels since she was writing in a cultural climate that did not accept direct opposition to the status quo. Only through an indirect critique could she publish views critical of the prevailing laws and conditions under which women of her time were forced to live.

By 1811, when *Sense and Sensibility* was published, an intense backlash against the women's rights fiction of the 1790s had made the publication of blatantly feminist works impossible in England. Yet the women's rights literature of fifteen to twenty years earlier had been very widely read and discussed, and many of the concepts explored in it continued to be in the minds of many of the writers of the early nineteenth century. Jane Austen was one such writer. In *Sense and Sensibility* she created a novel that explored the dangers to women of a society in which they were forced, by both law and custom, to rely on men for their very livelihoods. Women of the gentry, in particular, had little ability to become self-sufficient. Women like Elinor and Marianne Dashwood had few options other than reliance on men for support. Such a woman could become a governess if she were skilled enough. In such positions, however, most women earned very little and were often completely dependent upon the whims of the parents of their charges. Their position in society was also diminished; although a governess was not considered to be a servant in the same class as those who took care of the house and grounds, she was certainly not allowed to be on a social footing with her employers or their friends. As a result, a governess often lived a very solitary life. Women like the Dashwood sisters might also have the opportunity to become schoolteachers. But again, the salaries were very low and the work difficult, time-consuming, and often demeaning. Women who taught were rarely considered to be marriageable; thus working in such a profession, even temporarily, usually meant foregoing any possibility of marriage.

The most acceptable solution for a woman in the position of the Dashwoods or the Steeles was to marry, to find a husband who could provide for her support and sometimes the support of a spinster sister and/or widowed mother as well. Such a solution, however, prevented the woman from being self-sufficient. Once married, she became fully dependent upon her husband. In fact, even money belonging to a woman before marriage was no longer hers to control afterward. According to English common law, when a man and a woman were married, they became only one entity under the law. That one legal entity was the man. His wife legally became his property, much as were his minor children. A married woman could not legally control her own money, could not make business contracts, could, in fact, have no identity of her own under the law. This was known as the law of coverture. It was one of the many laws of England that the women's rights novels of the late eighteenth century vehemently opposed.

In *Sense and Sensibility* we do not see the main characters interacting after their marriages. The difficulties involved for women in the law of coverture may seem, therefore, not to be an issue in Austen's novel. But it is present—at the heart, in fact, of Marianne's story. The story of Colonel Brandon's first love, Eliza, is a story fit for any women's rights novel written by women's advocates such as Mary Wollstonecraft or Mary Hays. In it a young impressionable girl is forced into an arranged marriage she does not want by the man who, as her guardian, is responsible for taking care of her. Her husband is cruel to her, a cruelty that eventually drives her from his house. She has no recourse but to leave. Since she has no legal identity separate from that of her husband, she cannot divorce him—she cannot even appeal to the courts for a legal separation from him. Only a man has such rights. Her guardian, the one man who could legally act in her behalf, even after her marriage, is also the man who conspired with his son to place her in her untenable position. All the wealth she brought into her marriage is her husband's to control, legally and completely. And if she had had a child by him (which it appears she did not), he would have all parental rights to that child. A mother had no right even to her own child unless her husband granted it to her.

Austen does not lecture about the inequalities of the law towards men and women as she allows Brandon to tell Eliza's story. She doesn't need to. Anyone who had read such women's rights novels as Mary Wollstonecraft's *Maria, or the Wrongs of Woman* would recognize the similarities between Wollstonecraft's heroine and Austen's background story. Eliza's story does serve as a warning, however, that, as necessary as marriage was for the support of women like Elinor and Marianne Dashwood and Lucy and Anne Steele, it was also a danger. Choosing the right marital partner was essential since the laws of the land were fully on the side of husbands in any issue of importance in the England of Austen's time. Unlike some of her literary predecessors, Austen does not overtly preach feminism in any of her novels, but in each of them, the lack of adequate legal protection for women is a vital societal theme.

4

Pride and Prejudice
(1813)

Pride and Prejudice, the second novel Jane Austen published, is the best known of all of her novels. It was also her best-selling novel during her lifetime. The novel focuses on the Bennet family, a family of the lower gentry consisting of five daughters and their parents. The Bennets have little in the way of wealth beyond their home and the income which is connected to it, all of which will, when Mr. Bennet dies, be inherited by one of his distant cousins, Mr. Collins. Because of this inheritance, it is imperative that the young women of the household find husbands who can and will provide well for them, since their father is able to do very little to assure their future support and they have no brothers to take them in after their father's death.

Pride and Prejudice began its existence, like *Sense and Sensibility*, as an epistolary novel (see discussion of this form in Chapter 2) written when Austen was around twenty years of age. *First Impressions* was its original title. Although Austen thoroughly revised the novel over the next sixteen years or so before finding a publisher for it, the importance of "first impressions" remains strong in the published novel. The first impressions that many of the characters have about one another prove to be quite essential to the development of the plot as well as the development of the characters themselves.

The final version of *Pride and Prejudice*, published in 1813, was no longer written in epistolary style. Letters remain extremely important within the novel—especially those exchanged between Mr. Darcy and Elizabeth—but the narrative proceeds through use of a third-person narrator. Although that narrator shares the perspective of Elizabeth Bennet through much of the novel, it is, in fact, separate from her, enabling the narrator to comment on the actions and motives of characters much more objectively and thoroughly than could have been accomplished in a novel written as a series of letters among characters with no outside narrator.

When Austen wrote the original version of the story *First Impressions*, she was a young woman of an age to be courted and was probably considering marital options for herself. By the time she completed and published the final version of *Pride and Prejudice*, she was in her late thirties, a single woman dependent on the generosity of family and friends for her support, and well past her days of hopeful young courtship. The time lapse between her writing of *First Impressions* and her completion of the final version of *Pride and Prejudice* undoubtedly provided her with greater insights into the subject of courtship—its dangers, difficulties, pains, and foolishness, as well as its joy. All are displayed vividly in Austen's second published novel.

PLOT DEVELOPMENT

Pride and Prejudice begins with a line that is among the most famous opening lines in all of English literature: "It is a truth universally acknowledged, that a single man in possession of a good fortune, must be in want of a wife" (3). In essence, that opening sentence sets up the entire plot of the novel, which develops according to the following scenario. A man who has (or is thought to have) sufficient wealth to adequately support a wife arrives in the neighborhood. The women of the neighborhood then focus their attentions on determining which of the local young women would make the best wife for him and on encouraging a courtship between them. They also observe the competition for his hand and attempt to discourage his attentions to any other women. The movement of the plot in this novel is not, therefore, controlled by the men, but instead by the women. The task of the men is to avoid succumbing to such female machinations as would engage them in unhappy or inappropriate marriages as well as to recognize and pursue those marriages which have the possibility of providing them with a significant measure of happiness.

When the novel opens, Mr. and Mrs. Bennet are discussing the fact that the large estate in the neighborhood has been rented by Mr. Bingley, "a young man of large fortune from the north of England" (3). Upon hearing that Mr. Bingley is single, Mrs. Bennet exclaims: "A single man of large fortune; four or five thousand a year. What a fine thing for our girls!" (4). Mr. Bennet laughs at her and pretends not to understand what Mr. Bingley's fortune has to do with his daughters. But he understands his wife perfectly. As the narrator tells us, the "business of her life was to get her daughters married," a "business" in which it was necessary for many mothers of the period to engage themselves in order to protect their daughters from being left destitute and alone in the world (5).

Mr. Bingley has two sisters, Miss Bingley and Mrs. Hurst, both of whom moved to Netherfield with their brother. Mr. Hurst is also a member of the party, as is Mr. Bingley's longtime friend, Mr. Fitzwilliam Darcy. Mr. Darcy is also a man of wealth—of considerably more wealth, in fact, than his friend. He has already inherited a vast family estate in Derbyshire that has been in his family for many generations.

While Mrs. Bennet is setting her sights on winning Mr. Bingley and Mr. Darcy for two of her daughters, Mr. Bingley's sisters are intent on preventing any marriage between either wealthy bachelor and any fortuneless woman of the neighborhood. Miss Bingley has her own designs on Mr. Darcy, and neither of Mr. Bingley's sisters is willing to share their brother (and his wealth) with a new wife whom they may not be able to control. They too fully enjoy being mistresses of their brother's estate themselves to hand it over willingly to a prospective wife.

Through a series of visits between the neighboring families and a dance held at Netherfield, the Bennet family meets the Bingley party. Jane Bennet, the oldest of the five Bennet sisters, is immediately attracted to Mr. Bingley, as is he to her. They begin to spend considerable time together, encouraging the idea that they are, in fact, interested in more than an occasional dance with each other. Meanwhile, Elizabeth Bennet, the second oldest of the Bennet sisters, engages the attention of Mr. Darcy. They begin their interaction with a series of insults and slights, seeming to dislike each other intensely while, in fact, behaving in such ways precisely because of their mutual attraction.

While the Bennet sisters are of sufficient importance in the society of the English countryside to be included in the dances held at Netherfield, they are significantly below the social level of the Bingleys and *far* below the level of Mr. Darcy in greater English society. Thus when the attraction between Mr. Bingley and Jane Bennet seems about to move beyond the stage of flirtation, the Bingley sisters and Mr. Darcy convince Mr. Bingley to leave the neighborhood, assuming that by taking him away from Netherfield, the infatuation will dissipate and any danger of Mr. Bingley's lowering himself socially through an alliance with a woman of lower social standing than himself will be eliminated. According to a letter written to Elizabeth Bennet later in the novel by Mr. Darcy, neither he nor Mr. Bingley's sisters ever really consider Jane's feelings in their haste to remove Mr. Bingley from her influence. They assume that Jane simply recognizes a good catch when she sees one, and that when he is taken from her range of influence, she will merely place her attentions elsewhere. In fact, however, Jane Bennet is seriously in love with Mr. Bingley. She suffers greatly when he leaves the neighborhood, not even coming to say goodbye to her, as though their acquaintance has meant nothing at all to him.

Mr. Darcy is as anxious to withdraw himself from the neighborhood as he is to remove his friend. He finds himself drawn towards Elizabeth more and more—and, if her sister is not good enough socially for his friend, Mr. Bingley, Elizabeth is most certainly not of high enough rank socially for the wealthier and more established Mr. Darcy. By removing himself from the neighborhood, Mr. Darcy intends to remove both his friend and himself from the influence of the young women who attract them.

Social ranking is only one of the issues Mr. Darcy holds against the Bennets. Even more important is the behavior of certain members of the family. Mrs. Bennet knows how important it is to find suitable husbands for her daughters, but in her determination to marry them off, she behaves too obviously, too impulsively, and too coarsely to satisfy the sensibilities of a man like Mr. Darcy. Such behavior reflects on all of her daughters, not merely the younger ones who tend to follow her lead. This lack of propriety, along with the reminder in it of Mrs. Bennet's working-class origins (her marriage to Mr. Bennet raised her into the gentry), creates too large a chasm, socially, between the Bingley and Darcy levels of society and that of the Bennets for marriages between them to be seriously considered.

A more appropriate candidate for marriage with any one of the Bennet sisters arrives in the form of a distant cousin of their father, Mr. Collins. Mr. Collins is a clergyman, rector in the community of Rosings (the community in which Mr. Darcy's aunt, the Lady Catherine de Bourgh, is the leading landowner). Mr. Collins is the cousin who, by means of the entail on the Bennet's property Longbourne, will inherit it and the income it brings in when Mr. Bennet dies.

An entail was a legal device commonly used in eighteenth-century England. Through use of it, the owner of a property could control who inherited that property, not only immediately following him, but through several generations to come. Generally an entail was structured in such a way that the estate was passed down through the family from one eldest son in a family to the eldest son in the next generation, and so on, until the legal limit on its passage had been reached. If, however, an eldest son did not have a son, the estate then usually passed to the eldest nephew or male cousin in the next generation of the family.

Mr. Bennet, having no son to whom he could pass his estate, has no recourse but to leave it to his cousin, Mr. Collins. Knowing this, Mr. Collins, when he decides it is the appropriate time for him to marry, pays a visit to Longbourne with the intention of finding among his young cousins a suitable wife. "This," Austen tells us, "was his plan of amends—of atonement—for inheriting their father's estate; and he thought it an excellent one, full of eligibility and suitableness, and excessively generous and disinterested on his own part" (68). When Mr. Collins, finding that the eldest daughter is assumed by many in the neighborhood to be on the verge of becoming engaged to Mr. Bingley, turns his attentions to the second eldest daughter, Elizabeth, he is stunned and amazed to find her unwilling to accept the marital offer he so generously offers her. In fact, he has great difficulty believing her refusals, accusing her of playing coy with him, until finally she manages to convince him that she truly has no intention of accepting an offer that is not based on mutual love (101–107).

Mr. Collins does not suffer from his disappointment for long. A good friend of the Bennet girls, Charlotte Lucas, consoles Mr. Collins in his disappointment over Elizabeth's refusal and, in a short time, is proposed to herself and accepts the offer gratefully. Elizabeth finds Charlotte's decision to marry Mr. Collins reprehensible. She is unable to understand how a woman could deign to accept a marriage with someone with whom there is no shared love and few, if any, shared interests. But Charlotte, as the narrator assures us, "accepted him solely from the pure and disinterested desire of an establishment," a home of her own (119). At the age of twenty-seven, Charlotte knows she has little chance of finding the kind of love younger women like the Bennet girls dream of. She understands that she must marry and establish a home of her own. Otherwise she will be forced to live dependent on the generosity of her parents and brothers for the rest of her life. Marrying Mr. Collins seems a reasonable compromise, considering the alternatives.

The Collins's marriage is no less successful for being based on economics and suitability than are other marital relationships formed within the novel. In Charlotte, Mr. Collins finds a suitable partner who makes his home comfortable and who satisfies the desires of his patron and parishioners for a good rector's wife. In Mr. Collins, Charlotte finds a good provider who allows her to satisfy her desires for homemaking and serving her husband's patron and parishioners well. Elizabeth assumes at one point that Charlotte must tire of Mr. Collins's company from time to time—and asserts that this is the reason for Charlotte's choosing a dark, back room for her sitting room—but Charlotte never overtly signals any dissatisfaction with her fate. Mr. Collins is her "single man in possession of a good [enough] fortune," and she is pleased to have become the wife he must be "in want of" (3).

Another courtship of considerable importance in the novel is that of Lydia Bennet and the young militiaman, Wickham. Wickham is the son of Mr. Darcy's late father's estate manager. As a result, Darcy and Wickham grew up together, almost like brothers at times. Yet no two young men could be more different. While Mr. Darcy grew up to be a responsible young man who fulfilled his obligations to his parents, his sister, and the staff and tenants on his estate with great care, Wickham grew up to be a careless, selfish young man who resented the position and property that belonged to his childhood companion. When Mr. Darcy's sister, Georgiana, was just fifteen, Wickham convinced her to run away with him. He planned to compromise her, forcing himself in that way into the family and providing himself with access to the family fortune. The plot did not succeed, however, as Georgiana confided in her brother just two days before the planned elopement. Mr. Darcy prevented the two from running off together and forbade Wickham access to the Darcy family and estates thereafter.

The Bennets have no idea about Wickham's past when they meet him in town with a number of others from the militia. He courts Elizabeth quite openly, while, at the same time convincing the fifteen-year-old Lydia to run off with him secretly. He promises to take her to Scotland where they can marry without her parents' consent. Once they have run off, however, he postpones their trip to Scotland indefinitely. It seems unlikely that, barring the intercession of Lydia's family and friends, they would ever have married.

Mr. Bennet, his brother-in-law Mr. Gardiner, and Mr. Darcy combine their efforts and resources to track down Lydia and Wickham after they have run away together. They eventually find them in London and convince Wickham, through bribery, to marry Lydia, thus preventing her from becoming a completely disreputable and unmarriageable woman at such a young age. What could easily have become a major disaster for Lydia and the entire Bennet clan, therefore, is transformed into an inappropriate, but salvageable, interlude followed by an ill-advised, but acceptably happy marriage. Whereas the Collins's marriage is too suitable, appropriate, and disinterested for the taste of most readers, the Wickham marriage demonstrates the other extreme: a marriage unsuitable, inappropriate, and utterly based on individual self-interest and lust.

At the outset of the novel, we learn that the women of Netherfield and its neighborhood all assume that Mr. Bingley and Mr. Darcy must be "in want of a wife" (3). At that point, neither of the men seem to have given the prospect a great deal of thought. Miss Bingley clearly wants to attain the position of wife to Mr. Darcy, and Mr. Darcy's aunt, Lady Catherine de Bourgh, intends that he should marry her daughter. As for Mr. Bingley, those closest to him seem to feel that Georgiana Darcy might make a good marriage partner for him. But the men themselves enjoy their single status too much to give serious thought to their own nuptials. In the course of the novel, however, both men fall in love with women who are, ultimately, very well suited to them temperamentally, if not socially. While the two eldest Bennet girls are not the logical choices for these men according to societal standards of the day, they are ideal choices for marriages based on companionship and affection.

Jane and Elizabeth, unlike most of the women in their neighborhood, including those in their own family, do not consciously set out to win the hands of the two most eligible bachelors in the neighborhood. Jane Bennet and Mr. Bingley meet and find that they greatly enjoy each other's company. Their relationship develops emotionally, though they never express their growing affection openly. As a result, when Mr. Darcy and Mr. Bingley's sisters discourage the relationship and insist that Mr. Bingley leave the neighborhood with them, they are able to convince him that Jane does not feel as deeply for him as he had begun to expect that she had. Their relationship thus ends quite abruptly, and would probably never have recommenced had Elizabeth and Mr. Darcy never resumed their own communication.

Elizabeth Bennet and Fitzwilliam Darcy, on the other hand, do not begin their relationship with affectionate and positive feelings about each other. Mr. Darcy, recognizing the improprieties and coarseness of her family's behavior, wants nothing to do with Elizabeth when they first meet. Elizabeth, offended by Mr. Darcy's determination to insult her, is likewise repulsed initially by the idea of a more intimate relationship.

The relationship between Elizabeth and Mr. Darcy proceeds through a series of insults and misunderstandings. The attraction between them is clear—most of those around them see it distinctly—but the pair remains uncertain of each other's feelings throughout much of the novel, mostly as a result of misdirected pride.

Such a relationship would have been destined to fail had not others involved themselves in it. Lady Catherine de Bourgh, hearing the rumor that her nephew appeared to be falling into the clutches of a young woman with no fortune and significantly less social position than himself, visits Elizabeth to determine the accuracy of such rumors and to insist that Elizabeth have "such a report universally contradicted" (333). Lady Catherine declares that the rumor "*must* be a scandalous falsehood" (333). Elizabeth, however, even more unwilling to defer to Lady Catherine than she is to Mr. Darcy, refuses at first to deny an engagement between them. Lady Catherine tries to impress upon Elizabeth the fact that Mr. Darcy and her own daughter have been intended for each other by their parents since early childhood, hoping that such information will cause Elizabeth to back away from her nephew (335–336). But instead of retreating, Elizabeth claims that such a plan by parents would do nothing to deter her from an engagement with Mr. Darcy if, indeed, they were engaged. Lady Catherine insists that the lack of equal social standing between them should be sufficient to keep Elizabeth from accepting such a proposal, if Darcy actually made one. Elizabeth's own pride shines forth as she declares, "He is a gentleman; I am a gentleman's daughter; so far we are equal" (336). Finally, upon Lady Catherine's asking directly if Elizabeth is at present engaged to Fitzwilliam Darcy, Elizabeth responds that she is not. When asked, however, if she will promise "never to enter such an engagement," she responds: "I will make no promise of the kind" (336).

Lady Catherine leaves the Bennet home, disturbed and insulted by Elizabeth's refusal to defer to her. She tells her nephew of the behavior, assuming that such insubordination on the part of Elizabeth will turn Mr. Darcy away from her. In fact, however, the opposite is true. Because of the series of misunderstandings, disagreements, and overly-prideful exchanges between the potential marriage partners, Darcy has no idea that Elizabeth would even consider a permanent alliance with him. Upon hearing that she refused to promise Lady Catherine never to enter into an engagement with him, he begins to think about the prospect more seriously and to become hopeful that such an engagement could actually occur between them. When the prospective lovers are finally able to set aside the misunderstandings caused by their prideful natures, true communication between them finally becomes possible. They discover their mutual love and marry each other, quite happily, by the end of the novel.

CHARACTER DEVELOPMENT

The majority of the characters in *Pride and Prejudice* can be best understood by examining them in relation to their prospective and actual marriage partners. Individually the characters are well-developed, but by evaluating their behaviors and attitudes in relation to those men and women with whom they form a lifetime partnership, their characters come much more fully alive than they otherwise would. By examining the relationships of couples such as Mr. and Mrs. Bennet, Lydia Bennet and Wickham, and Elizabeth Bennet and Mr. Darcy, the intricacies of each individual character become more vivid.

Mr. Bennet is an intelligent gentleman who enjoys spending time alone in his library more than any other activity. Of his five daughters, his favorite is Elizabeth, a young woman with a great deal of intelligence and passion for life. His wife, on the other hand, lacks the kind of intelligence he prizes, talks incessantly on inappropriate subjects, and reveals her lack of breeding in almost every action she takes. The narrator explains that Mr. Bennet,

captivated by youth and beauty, and that appearance of good humour, which youth and beauty generally give, had married a woman whose weak understanding and illiberal mind, had very early in their marriage put an end to all real affection for her. Respect, esteem, and confidence, had vanished for ever; and all his views of domestic happiness were overthrown. (223)

Mr. Bennet's choice of a marriage partner was, indeed, foolish, but rather than attempt to educate her—or at the very least, to guide her in ways that would prevent her from embarrassing him and the rest of the family—Mr. Bennet locks himself into his library at every opportunity, choosing thereby to avoid contact with his wife as much as possible. Such separation from her enables her to run the house and raise her children as inappropriately as she chooses, with little input from her more intelligent husband. But his constant separation from the household is not the worst of his behaviors. He also derides and ridicules his wife, sometimes to her face, sometimes behind her back, but often in front of their children. Elizabeth recognizes her father's faulty behavior: She

had never been blind to the impropriety of her father's behaviour as a husband. She had always seen it with pain; but respecting his abilities, and grateful for his affectionate treatment of herself, she endeavoured to forget what she could not overlook, and to banish from her thoughts that continual breach of conjugal obligation and decorum which, in exposing his wife to the contempt of her own children, was so highly reprehensible. (224)

For a man to show disrespect towards his wife so often and thoroughly, especially in front of their children, reveals much about the man's character. His foolishness did not end with his youthful indiscretion; it continues throughout his marriage as he neglects to provide his wife and daughters with the guidance they need from him.

The character of Lydia Bennet Wickham is likewise most fully developed in relation to that of her husband. Early in the novel, Lydia and Kitty are seen following after various of the militiamen in town. They admit to having their heads turned by uniforms and to being fascinated by the soldiers in general. They, like their mother, demonstrate little discretion and discernment. They appear, however, to be very open and honest young women, despite their inappropriate behavior. Only in her relationship with Wickham does Lydia reveal the fullness of her ability for secretiveness and deceit. She knows her parents would disapprove of the seriousness of her relationship with Wickham, so when asking their permission to go to Brighton with a friend, she does not reveal that Wickham's presence in Brighton is one of her primary motivations for going there. She secretly plots with Wickham to run off to Scotland, where she believes they will be married without parental approval. But Wickham does not take her directly to Scotland; instead he lives with her in London without benefit of marriage. When her father, uncle, and Mr. Darcy find them and force Wickham to marry her, she feels no remorse about her behavior. In fact, when she returns to Longbourne with her husband for a visit, she behaves as though there is nothing improper or indecent about the circumstances of her marriage. For a woman of Austen's time to feel no guilt, remorse, or embarrassment over being seduced and living with a man outside of marriage would have been a sign of just how low she had sunk, ethically speaking.

Wickham, of course, was a partner suited to her behavior. Not only had he attempted to seduce and ruin Georgiana Darcy earlier in his life, but he had succeeded in seducing Lydia and taking her away from her family and friends. His intent seems never to have been to marry her, and he only does so when offered a substantial amount of money by her family and friends contingent on the marriage. Yet he, like Lydia, shows no remorse, guilt, or embarrassment over his situation. If one had no knowledge of his behavior with both Lydia and Georgiana, one might well think him merely a handsome, rather foolish, young soldier who is an easy charmer and smooth talker. His behavior with these two young women, however, clarifies just how fully a scoundrel he really is.

Mr. Fitzwilliam Darcy's character is, perhaps, the most difficult to grasp in its fullness, especially in the early part of the story. Part of that difficulty comes from the fact that much of the story is seen from the perspective of Elizabeth Bennet, and she remains confused by him until late in the story. But the use of Elizabeth's perspective is not the only source of confusion for Mr. Darcy's character. He, more than any other character in the novel, behaves differently depending upon the location of the action and the position of the people he interacts with in that location. As Elizabeth learns more about Mr. Darcy through a combination of direct observation and hearing stories about him, she comes to understand the intricate nature of his personality more fully. And the reader, by learning these various aspects of his personality along with Elizabeth, as well as by observing the development of his relationship with her, comes to know Mr. Darcy much more thoroughly than would be possible otherwise.

Elizabeth observes Mr. Darcy's prideful behavior at the outset of the novel when he is forced by circumstances to associate with those in the neighborhood of Netherfield whom he believes to be beneath him in both social position and understanding. She watches him behave as though his opinion is always the right one, separating Mr. Bingley from the woman he is growing to love merely because he believes Jane Bennet is not of high enough social standing for his friend. She observes his hesitance about asking for her own hand in marriage once he has fallen in love with her, a hesitance resulting from the fact that he does not want to be associated with her parents and younger sisters, all of whom he knows himself to be vastly superior to. These observed behaviors encourage Elizabeth to question the wisdom of her attraction to him; a man who could behave in such ways could be an insufferably elitist husband who might never let her forget how his willingness to condescend saved her from a life of poverty and drudgery with those much less worthy than himself. But fortunately Elizabeth's knowledge of Mr. Darcy's true character does not come only from her own experience of him; she also has access to stories told about him from those who know him well.

The first stories that Elizabeth hears about Mr. Darcy are from Wickham who tells her his version of their relationship. Wickham, of course, makes Darcy the villain of the piece, suggesting that he had refused to follow his own father's directions to help Wickham into the profession of his choice. His version of the story presents Mr. Darcy as a spiteful, selfish individual, a presentation that Elizabeth is prone to accept at that point in her relationship with the young aristocrat due to her personal experience of his prideful behavior. Later information forces her to question the veracity of Wickham's version of the events.

Elizabeth hears the most important story about Mr. Darcy when she and her aunt and uncle, the Gardiners, visit the Darcy estate, Pemberley, in Derbyshire. Mrs. Reynolds, the housekeeper at Pemberley for many years, speaks glowingly of her young master to the visitors: "I have never had a cross word from him in my life, and I have known him ever since he was four years old" (232). When Mr. Gardiner remarks on Mrs. Reynolds's luck in working for such a person, Mrs. Reynolds replies: "If I was to go through the world, I could not meet with a better" (233). Mrs. Reynolds discusses her master's reputation throughout the neighborhood of Pemberley: "He is the best landlord, and the best master . . . that ever lived. Not like the wild young men now-a-days, who think of nothing but themselves. There is not one of his tenants or servants but what will give him a good name" (233). She admits that "[s]ome people call him proud," but claims never to have seen "any thing of it" (233). And her assessment of her master's "good name" is corroborated by others in the neighborhood.

That the housekeeper for the estate who has been in residence for the whole of Mr. Darcy's life would discuss his character in such glowing terms gives Elizabeth pause. She finds herself questioning both her own perceptions and the story relayed by Wickham in light of Mrs. Reynolds's revelations. Only after she visits Pemberley and hears Mrs. Reynolds's stories of Mr. Darcy's life is Elizabeth willing to give him a fair chance. She is then willing to consider his attentions to her from a less defensive, more open-minded position.

Just as we learn the intricacies of Mr. Darcy's character through Elizabeth's analysis of her own observations together with the stories she hears about him, so do we become better acquainted with Elizabeth than we would otherwise be able to by observing her interaction with Mr. Darcy. Watching Elizabeth with her family, we are assured of her superior intellect and sense of propriety, but we do not observe the excesses of her own pride and her tendency to prejudge others until we observe her in relation to Mr. Darcy. She is understandably hurt when she overhears Mr. Darcy telling Mr. Bingley that she is "tolerable," though not worthy of his attentions (9). But she decides that she understands his character completely, based on the single comment. In other words, she operates on the principle of prejudice—prejudging a person based on insufficient information about them. Once she has decided that she understands his character, she tends to judge all of his words and actions according to her first impression, her initial prejudice against him. It is not until she has accumulated a remarkable amount of information that counters her first impression that she is willing to reconsider her position, in time growing to love him, trust him, and ultimately marry him.

Both Elizabeth Bennet and Fitzwilliam Darcy rely initially on first impressions (the original title of the novel). But by the end of the novel they have both been forced to reexamine their initial assumptions and revise their opinions based on the facts before them. Both grow and change before our eyes, developing into strong individuals who have a tremendous possibility of happiness in their lives together as a well-suited couple.

THEMATIC ISSUES

Just as "Sense" and "Sensibility" are linked both in the title and thematically, so are "Pride" and "Prejudice" linked in Jane Austen's second published novel. "Sense" and "Sensibility" are both depicted as qualities that each character needs in proper balance. "Pride" and "Prejudice," on the other hand, are potentially dangerous qualities that Fitzwilliam Darcy and Elizabeth Bennet must overcome or avoid if they are to build a successful life together.

Although Mr. Darcy is often referred to in the novel as prideful, pride is not his failing. He appreciates his heritage and wants to live up to it, but he does not lord the position he holds over other people. As Mrs. Reynolds points out, "[s]ome people call him proud," but she has never seen him display unseemly pride to her, to the other staff members, or to anyone in the neighborhood of Pemberley (233). Instead, Mr. Darcy's most serious failing is his prejudice. According to Samuel Johnson's 1755 *Dictionary of the English Language*, the first definition of prejudice in Austen's time was a "prepossession; a judgment formed beforehand with examination." Darcy prejudges those around him based on minimal contact with them combined with the behavior of their relations. He considers Jane Bennet to be an inappropriate marriage partner for his friend Bingley because of the behavior of her mother and younger sister, ignoring the fact that Jane, herself, behaves appropriately. He also jumps to the conclusion that Jane cares for Bingley more as a meal ticket than as a man because of his prejudices against women of her class; women, he assumes, must be more interested in marrying for money than for love. His prejudices catch up with him, however, when he finds himself falling in love with Elizabeth. She and Jane belong to the same class, even to the same family. If he is to accept the fact that he and Elizabeth would be a reasonable match, he must face his prejudices and conquer them. He must admit that he was wrong to judge Jane on the basis of her social position and family connections. He must recognize the need to judge individuals as individuals, not as members of particular groups of people.

Elizabeth Bennet also forms judgments based on too little information. Her initial prejudice against Mr. Darcy is based on minimal exposure to him in an environment that is not familiar to or comfortable for him. Not until she visits Pemberley, the Darcy estate, and talks with the housekeeper, Mrs. Reynolds, does Elizabeth begin to discern Mr. Darcy's true character. At that point she has finally gathered sufficient information to begin to judge him accurately and responsibly.

Mr. Darcy and Elizabeth are both proud of their individual heritages. Elizabeth is as proud of having been born the daughter of a gentleman as Mr. Darcy is to have been born the only son of a very wealthy and proud landowner. Their pride in their positions is not, however, excessive. Had it been so, it is unlikely they could ever have convinced themselves to seriously consider marriage with one another—Mr. Darcy because he would not have been willing to marry beneath him in wealth and social position, and Elizabeth because she would not have allowed herself to be placed in the position of needing to be grateful to a man of Mr. Darcy's stature. The primary example of excessive pride in the novel is Lady Catherine de Bourgh, a woman who cannot tolerate the idea of her nephew marrying the daughter of a minor gentleman who cannot supply her with a decent marriage settlement. Such excessive pride prevents her from developing close bonds of friendship with anyone, since she considers everyone only from the perspective of how they reflect upon her own position in society.

The primary theme of *Pride and Prejudice* is not, however, reflected in its title. Instead, *Pride and Prejudice* is a novel that focuses on courtship and marriage. As such, it explores a range of the kinds of marriages available to people of the gentry and aristocratic classes in the early nineteenth century as well as the importance of adherence to propriety and duty in order to create and maintain happy and productive marriages.

The marriage of Mr. and Mrs. Bennet illustrates the kind of marriage which, though based on affection and attraction, can never be successful. Mr. Bennet was not very discerning about the true nature of his young love's personality. He was attracted to her beauty and vitality, without, it appears, ever questioning her lack of intellectual and household management skills. But beyond his lack of discernment at the time of the marriage, Mr. Bennet fails to fulfill his duties to his wife, family, and position throughout his lifetime. His responsibilities include caring for them, making certain that they will be provided for after his death, and taking care that his daughters are raised to be proper young ladies with good morals and a proper sense of propriety. These duties he chooses not to fulfill. Had he taken a more active role in the organization and management of the household from the beginning, he might have been able to put aside significant amounts of income for his daughters' future. He might also have been able to teach his wife and daughters how to behave with decorum and propriety at all times.

The marriage of Charlotte Lucas and Mr. Collins represents marriage based on economics and mutual comfort. When Mr. Collins visits Longbourne, he comes with the objective of finding a wife. He has no expectation of falling in love—love has no place in his expectations of happiness in setting up a household. His is to be a marriage of suitability and of appropriateness, not of love and affection. He is looking for a woman who will match his social status, who will function well as the wife of a rector, and who will fit comfortably into a life at Longbourne after Mr. Bennet dies. Such a plan is far from the companionate marriages based on love that women like Jane and Elizabeth Bennet dream of. Charlotte Lucas, however, a woman who, at the age of twenty-seven, is facing the very likely possibility of never having a home of her own, is pleased with Mr. Collins's offer of such a marriage. In it, the duty of the husband is to provide a stable home for his wife and any children born of the marriage. The wife's duty is to maintain the home well while providing for her husband's comfort and the proper education of any children born to them. Passion is not expected, although, in reality, many marriages formed in this way did result in a growing love and passion between the partners. By twenty-first-century standards, such a marriage may seem cold, even mercenary, but in eighteenth-century England, such marriages were more common (and generally more commonly approved of) than those based on love and affection.

The marriage of Elizabeth Bennet and Fitzwilliam Darcy represents the affectionate and companionate marriage at its best. Numerous circumstances conspired to make their finding and committing to each other quite unlikely. First, their social statuses were significantly different, Mr. Darcy being a member of the landed aristocracy and Elizabeth Bennet being a fortuneless girl born to a man of gentry status. Second, the distance between their homes was considerable. Had Mr. Darcy's friend not rented a home in the neighborhood of the Bennets, little likelihood exists that the two would ever have had the opportunity to meet. Even if, for instance, they were both in London or one of the resort towns of England at the same time, the difference in their social status would most likely have kept them from attending the same social functions.

Once they did meet, however, the obstacles to their future together were by no means over. Other people then present obstacles to their engagement. The lack of propriety and decorum demonstrated by Elizabeth's mother and sisters causes Mr. Darcy to dread any connection with them. And the women in Mr. Darcy's life (his aunt and the Bingley sisters, in particular) do everything they can to prevent any alliance between Elizabeth and the man she is growing to love. But despite all obstacles, Elizabeth and Mr. Darcy do find each other and commit to each other for life.

In their marriage, as in their courtship, the pair continue to spar with each other verbally, demonstrating an openness of heart and growing ease of temper which allow them to treat each other as equals in respect and honor. Both adhere to their individual duties within the marriage, but they seem to be able to share much more than would be likely in marriages such as Mr. and Mrs. Bennet's or Mr. and Mrs. Collins's. The affectionate, companionate marriage, if operated in accordance with duty and propriety, Austen seems to infer, is the one best suited to the happiness of all concerned.

HISTORICAL CONTEXT: INHERITANCE LAW

Jane Austen had a strong interest in the situation of the entailment of estates and the effects of that entailment (and of the legal principle of primogeniture on which entailment was based) on family members. Both *Sense and Sensibility* and *Pride and Prejudice* deal overtly with issues of entailment. Primogeniture, the inheritance by the eldest son of all the property belonging to a family, is an important thematic issue in each of Austen's completed novels.

An entailment, also known as strict settlement, was a legal device commonly used in seventeenth- and eighteenth-century England by the owner of a property to protect the integrity of that property for several generations into the future. The way it worked was as follows: The person who owned the property outright could devise by his will or a settlement drawn up separately that his property would be inherited, intact, through the generations living at the time of his death, plus one. In other words, if a man (it was almost never a woman) who owned an estate lived to see his son, his grandson, and his great-grandson born, the strict settlement could (and usually did) declare that the estate must pass through the family, in that order, finally settling on the great-great-grandson that had not yet been born when the settlement was originally written. Once the original owner died, each succeeding owner would only have the right to the use of the estate, not an outright ownership of it. He could live on the estate, collect rents from any tenants that might live on the estate, and use the income from the estate to maintain the estate itself as well as to provide for his family. He was not allowed, however, to sell the estate or any part thereof or to detract from the value of the estate in any way. He was required to keep it intact and in good order for the next generation.

Note that I use the pronoun "he" throughout this description of entailment. Legally there was no barrier to leaving an estate to women—even using strict settlement as a means of doing so. But in practice, such inheritance was extremely rare. The common law of England required that, in cases where a will was not left and an entailment was not in force, an estate was to be inherited automatically by the eldest son of a family. If there were no sons, it would be inherited, in equal portions, by all the daughters of the family. This is the law of primogeniture. As a result of that law and the customs that grew up around it, women and younger sons rarely received substantial inheritances from their fathers. Estates remained intact, ostensibly to protect the family and the family property as a whole, but only the eldest sons had much say about the manner in which estate income and property was to be used.

An Economic Reading of *Pride and Prejudice*

Financial status and the operations of inheritance play a fundamental role in *Pride and Prejudice*. One might almost consider the entailment on Longbourne to be a character in the novel, never speaking openly, but always present, determining actions and consequences for many of the individuals within the novel. By examining *Pride and Prejudice* from an economic perspective, readers can more clearly understand the plot device of the entail as well as many other thematic issues in the novel. Economic interpretations of literature often reveal the power base of the society on which the novel is built as well as the author's own view about the appropriateness of that power base. By examining the economic structure of Austen's fictional world in *Pride and Prejudice*, the reader can interpret numerous aspects of the novel more fully than would otherwise be possible.

Economics is at the core of *Pride and Prejudice*. Mr. Bennet, never having had a son, is unable to use his property to provide for his family after his death since one of the stipulations included in most legal entailments was that, if there were no son to inherit the property, it would descend to the eldest nephew or male cousin in the next generation of the family. Mr. Collins is that individual. Mrs. Bennet rages against the entail and blames her husband for not having found some way to break its hold on the property. While the novel encourages the readers to see Mrs. Bennet's fury as a part of her general silliness, that fury does have some basis in justice. She insists to her husband that "it is the hardest thing in the world, that your estate should be entailed away from your own children" and suggests that she would have done something about it "long ago" if she had been he (60). The narrator informs us that Jane and Elizabeth tried, once again as they had many times before, to explain the legalities involved in an entail, "but it was a subject on which Mrs. Bennet was beyond the reach of reason; and she continued to rail bitterly against the cruelty of settling an estate away from a family of five daughters" (60). Jane and Elizabeth try to explain the facts to their mother, emphasizing the way things are. But Mrs. Bennet is not really arguing about the way things are—she is fully aware that she and her daughters will be turned out of their home immediately upon the death of her husband. What Mrs. Bennet argues about is the way things *should* be. It *is* cruel to settle an estate away from five daughters who have very little money to share among themselves. It *does* seem unfair that a person can inherit an estate merely on the basis of being born the oldest male in an individual family or, even more unfairly, by being born the eldest male in a particular generation of a barely known branch of the extended family. Primogeniture does favor men over women and elder brothers over their siblings. On this point, the reader must agree with Mrs. Bennet, silly though she is in many ways.

By the end of the novel the Bennet women no longer have any financial worries. Marriage into the Bingley and Darcy families guarantees that all of the women will be cared for financially. But the fact that Austen does not leave the reader with women leading destitute and unpleasant lives does not remove the criticism of the system of entailment that is at the heart of the novel. Had Jane and Elizabeth not married well, the best that the Bennet girls could expect would be to marry a clergyman or soldier who might be able to provide them with roofs over their heads and sufficient food, but little more. And if they did not marry, they would have been likely to have slipped down the social ladder until they were living in rented rooms, relying on neighbors and distant relatives to assist them from time to time, like the Bates women in Austen's next novel, *Emma*. Had Longbourne not been entailed as it was, the Bennet women would never have been faced with the prospect of falling into such poverty and dependence.

5

Mansfield Park
(1814)

Jane Austen began her third novel, *Mansfield Park*, in 1811. It was the first novel that she both started and completed while living at Chawton Cottage, the home provided by her brother Edward a few years after her father's death. Her earlier novels, *Sense and Sensibility* and *Pride and Prejudice*, had been revised for publication at Chawton, but Austen began writing both of them during her early years at Steventon. *Mansfield Park*, therefore, is the first novel both conceived and entirely written by the mature Jane Austen. *Mansfield Park* combines a rather prudish and initially unattractive heroine with a story line that includes discussions of serious issues such as ordination, adultery, and the effects of environmental influences on the individual. This approach creates a novel that differs greatly in tone from Austen's first two publications.

Reactions to the first publication of *Mansfield Park* tended to be very strong. Many readers were extremely pleased that Austen had written a novel that focused attention on the importance of moral behavior and that so vehemently criticized the corruption that was so prevalent among many in England's royalty and aristocracy at the time. Many of those readers saw the behavior of the Crawfords, and Maria and Tom Bertram as reflections of the behavior of the Royal Princes, Princess, and their companions. The Prince Regent and his brother the Duke of Clarence both lived openly with mistresses. The Duke and his mistress, Mrs. Jordan, had ten children together before he turned her out. The Prince Regent, although married, was rarely seen in the company of his wife, choosing instead to have his mistress as his public hostess as well as his daily companion. Even Princess Charlotte's lifestyle reflected the general decadence and moral corruption of the younger members of the Court. She spent much of her time and energy flirting openly with inappropriate men, including her own cousin, the eldest son of the Duke of Clarence and Mrs. Jordan (Tomalin 224). Many among the English resented the behavior of the Royals. Austen's readers who held this view were grateful to have such ethical issues handled in so uncompromising a manner.

Other readers responded quite differently. In her biography of Austen, Claire Tomalin details the family reaction:

Rather than praising the high moral tone, her mother found the virtuous heroine "insipid." Anna [Austen's niece] also declared that she "could not bear Fanny." Edward's son George [Austen's nephew] disliked Fanny too, and much preferred Mary Crawford. . . . As for Cassandra [Austen's sister], although she was "fond of Fanny," she also, according to one of her nieces, tried to persuade Jane to let her marry Henry Crawford; which suggests that the "moral tendency" so much admired by other readers did not impress her much. (225–226)

Many readers, both in Austen's lifetime and in the two hundred years since, have agreed with these family reactions. The most lively and interesting characters throughout much of the novel are Mary and Henry Crawford, the brother and sister pair who present Fanny and Edmund with the most difficult moral dilemmas. Mary is fun-loving, charming, and attractive. She also appears to have a good heart, even though many of her ideas are morally suspect. Henry is likewise fun-loving and charming. He is handsome and carries himself with confidence. Both Mary and Henry enjoy flirtations, even morally suspect ones. But Henry, like his sister, seems to have a good heart, as is evidenced by his genuine affection for and interest in Fanny. Fanny and Edmund, the heroine and hero of the book, are much less attractive characters, at least on the surface. Fanny is not a traditional heroine; instead she is quiet, shy, plain, and even somewhat priggish. Edmund has an admirable allegiance to duty and family, but for readers of Austen's time who were more accustomed to heroes who had a change of heart after a somewhat wild youth, Edmund was generally less appealing than Henry Crawford.

Debate over the place of *Mansfield Park* in Austen's work continues to the present day. It is often referred to as her "problem novel," a novel that does not allow for easy interpretation due to the strong contradictory feelings it arouses in so many readers. Even today readers tend to either love Fanny or to detest her, to consider Austen's ending to the novel absolutely appropriate or to see it as completely wrongheaded and forced. *Mansfield Park* has generated a larger number of contradictory interpretations and opinions in print than any other of Austen's novels.

PLOT DEVELOPMENT

Mansfield Park opens with an introduction to three sisters. The first is Miss Maria Ward of Huntingdon, who "with only seven thousand pounds, had the good luck to captivate Sir Thomas Bertram, of Mansfield Park, in the country of Northampton, and to be thereby raised to the rank of a baronet's lady, with all the comforts and consequences of a handsome house and large income" (Vol. I, 5). Her eldest sister, not as fortunate, "found herself" after several years of seeking a man of similar fortune, "obliged to be attached to the Rev. Mr. Norris, a friend of her brother-in-law, with scarcely any private fortune" (Vol I, 6). Mr. Norris was granted the position of rector in the Bertram's neighborhood. As a result, Mrs. Norris sees Lady Bertram on a daily basis. The third sister, Miss Frances Ward, was the least fortunate. She "married, in the common phrase, to disoblige her family, and by fixing on [Mr. Price,] a Lieutenant of Marines, without education, fortune, or connections, did it very thoroughly" (Vol I, 6). She lives in Portsmouth, far from her sisters in both distance and social position.

As the story begins, Mrs. Price, expecting her ninth child, writes her sister, Lady Bertram, in an attempt to be reconciled with her family and to receive promises of assistance from Lady Bertram for her children's futures. The narrator informs us that it "re-established peace and kindness. Sir Thomas sent friendly advice and professions, Lady Bertram despatched money and baby-linen, and Mrs. Norris wrote the letters" (Vol. I, 8). Upon further consideration of what they might do for Mrs. Price, Mrs. Norris conceives of a plan to take one of the Price children to be raised by herself and her sister at Mansfield. By doing so, she suggests, they can relieve the Price family of the expense and care of one child and can, with little trouble or expense to themselves, provide the child with a better education and introduction to society than she can receive in her parents' home. So develops the plan for Fanny Price to come to Mansfield Park to be raised with her cousins.

Fanny's parents approve of the plan immediately, and Fanny, at the age of only nine years old, leaves the only home she has ever known to join the Bertram household. She is to be educated and raised with her cousins, but she will also be constantly reminded of her place as a dependent cousin. Her room is an attic room, near that of the governess, rather than a room suitable for one of her cousins. She is taught alongside her female cousins, provided with essentially the same education, though not accorded any special training suited to her specific talents. She is allowed to ride when a suitable horse is available for her, but she does not have access to a horse of her own. She is expected, as a dependent niece, to make herself useful, keeping Lady Bertram company when no one else wants to do so and running errands for Mrs. Norris whenever she asks. Fanny's time is not her own.

Fanny has four cousins. Maria and Julia Bertram are the female cousins with whom she is educated. They pay her little attention, understanding the "distinction" between their position and hers much too well and treating her as their Aunt Norris does, as a poor relation who deserves little attention or respect. Tom Bertram, the eldest son and heir apparent to the family estate, is several years older than his cousin and is away from home for much of Fanny's youth. He is never intentionally cruel to her, but his selfishness does, at times, cause her considerable discomfort. Edmund Bertram, the younger son destined for a career as a clergyman, is the cousin closest to Fanny in temperament and moral sensibility. Edmund becomes her one true friend at Mansfield Park.

Within the novel, the behavior of each of the Bertram children is viewed from the perspective of Fanny, the representative of moral certitude as well as the central consciousness through which most of the story is filtered. The fact that all of her cousins except Edmund ignore their younger cousin, rather than make of her a confidante or friend, results in Fanny being able to observe her cousins' behaviors more objectively than she might otherwise. For example, when Tom Bertram decides to produce the play *Lovers' Vows* at Mansfield Park, Fanny is horrified. She knows that his father, who is away in the Americas handling family business, would not approve such a plan if he were home. She also recognizes the extreme impropriety of spending time, energy, and money on such an activity at the very time that Sir Thomas may be making a dangerous ocean crossing. Such objections to putting on a family theatrical may seem overly cautious, but Fanny is not the only person at Mansfield Park to feel such behavior improper. Edmund Bertram also protests against his siblings and friends producing a play, especially the kind of play they are considering, filled with improper relationships and requiring the actors playing those parts to interact inappropriately.

Tom Bertram ignores the recommendations of his brother and cousin, claiming that, as the future owner of Mansfield Park, he has the right to use it as he sees fit. His sister Maria, knowing that she will play the lead female character opposite Henry Crawford, a young man she is attracted to (despite her engagement to Mr. Rushworth), supports Tom in his decision to proceed with the play. Julia, who is also attracted to Henry Crawford and who, as the unattached sister, seems to have more right than her sister to his attentions, withdraws from the play. Her withdrawal, however, has nothing to do with morality or propriety; it results from a fit of pique at her sister for monopolizing Henry's attentions.

Henry's sister, Mary Crawford, also decides to perform. The character she chooses is one of another pair of young lovers, and she very much wants Edmund, to whom she is attracted, to play opposite her. Knowing that Edmund is against mounting the production, Mary and Tom explain that they will have to involve at least one other neighborhood family if Edmund doesn't perform. Edmund, concerned for Mary's feelings at being forced to act the part of a lover to a virtual stranger and determined to prevent the expansion of the project to include a young man none of them know well, decides that he must act in the play, despite his objections to it. He asks Fanny for advice. Fanny refuses to support Edmund's allowing himself to be "drawn in to do what [he] had resolved against, and what [he is] known to think will be disagreeable" to his father (Vol. I, 203). But she cannot convince him to give up his plan to act in the play. His rationale is that, by doing so, he can prevent the circle of those involved from becoming even larger and that he can prevent Mary Crawford from having to suffer acting the lover with a man she barely knows. But Fanny knows, based on her observation of him with Mary and on the language he uses about her, that the fundamental reason for his change of mind is his attraction to Mary Crawford. He is not, therefore, merely *appearing* to be inconsistent, as he proclaims; he *is* inconsistent, following the dictates of his heart rather than his personal ethics.

As rehearsals for the play progress, Fanny observes that the relationship between Maria and Henry is deepening, that even Mr. Rushworth, who tends to be oblivious to any kind of subtlety, is uncomfortable about the closeness between his fiancée and the young man playing the part of her lover. Maria, who is more interested in her future husband's estate than his personality, is fascinated by the charming Henry and uses rehearsals of the play to create opportunities for them to be alone together.

Mary and Edmund also rehearse their parts. Their relationship deepens as well, with Edmund overlooking Mary's lapses of propriety as he grows more and more infatuated with her, and with Mary trying to avoid the thought that Edmund is destined to become a country clergyman, a position for which she has little respect. Fanny's observations of the couple enable her to see the shallowness of Mary's moral sensibilities as well as the ways in which Edmund compromises his own sense of propriety and morality for Mary.

Shortly before the play is scheduled to be performed, Sir Thomas arrives home, unexpectedly and ahead of schedule. He is, as Fanny and Edmund have foreseen, horrified by the state of things. He disapproves of family theatricals in any form; he is outraged that several rooms in the house, including his own private study, have been disrupted for the sets and props; and he deplores the fact that his home is filled with strangers when he wants only the peace and comfort of his family around him. The play *Lovers' Vows* is never performed, but the damage has been done. The relationship between Maria and Henry has developed to the point at which it is clear that Maria will never be happy as the wife of Mr. Rushworth, a man without the charm or sensibilities of Henry Crawford. And Edmund is smitten as well, with a young woman who could never be content as the wife of a plain country clergyman.

Maria Bertram, unwilling to give up a future as the mistress of Rushworth's great estate, Sotherton, and uncertain about the depth of Henry Crawford's feelings for her, marries Mr. Rushworth despite her lack of interest in him as an individual. The Rushworths, accompanied by Maria's sister Julia, go off after the wedding to stay for a time in the resort town of Brighton.

Meanwhile, Fanny remains the only female of marriageable age at Mansfield Park. Henry Crawford, having no one else to flirt with, decides to flirt with her. "[M]y plan" he tells his sister, "is to make Fanny Price in love with me" (Vol. I, 297). Henry insists that he "cannot be satisfied without Fanny Price, without making a small hole in Fanny Price's heart" (Vol. I, 297).

Fanny, having observed Henry's previous courting of her cousins and understanding that, for Henry, the enjoyment is in the conquering of a woman's heart rather than in a commitment to her, distrusts his attentions. She has no interest in a man with such a dubious sense of right and wrong. But she is also protected from Henry's charm by the fact that her heart is already attached. She has loved her cousin Edmund for years, and while she does not expect him to return her love in kind, she cannot consider loving any other man in the same way. Her heart is, therefore, protected from the machinations of Henry Crawford in two ways: by her clear ethical center and by the fact that her heart already belongs to another man.

Henry's emotions, on the other hand, have no such protection. The more he courts Fanny, the more impressed he is with her. He decides that he is no longer merely trying to win her heart as a game of conquest, but that she is the woman he wants to commit to for life. Henry decides to give what assistance he can to Fanny's favorite brother, William, who has been waiting for some time to get promoted in the Navy. Since Henry's uncle is an admiral, he introduces William to him and encourages his uncle to arrange for William's promotion. Fanny is immensely grateful for Henry's assistance but remains skeptical of his ability to change from the scheming, inconsistent man he has been for so long.

Henry's attentions to Fanny do not go unnoticed elsewhere in the Bertram household. Edmund observes Henry's behavior and encourages his cousin to consider Henry's suit seriously. A marriage between Henry and Fanny would, Edmund surmises, help him to win Mary Crawford, as future interaction between the families would be assured were there a marriage between them. Sir Thomas likewise observes Henry's attentions towards Fanny. He, unaware of Henry's indecorous behavior towards Maria, encourages the relationship. That

Fanny might find a husband who could provide for her as well as a man with Henry's fortune could seems to him to be an advantage that the penniless Fanny cannot afford to refuse.

Henry, according to tradition and propriety, approaches Sir Thomas for permission to propose to his niece. Sir Thomas quite happily grants it. Upon later hearing that Fanny has refused Henry's offer, he becomes quite confused, frustrated, and even angry. He accuses Fanny of ingratitude to himself and his family as well as Henry. To punish Fanny for her ingratitude, Sir Thomas sends her for an extended visit to her parents' home in Portsmouth, a place she has not visited since she left it at the age of nine. She is initially excited by the prospect of seeing her parents and siblings again, but upon arriving at their home, she discovers just how different the life she leads at Mansfield Park is from that of her Portsmouth family. The family home is tiny, with several children occupying each bedroom and no privacy anywhere. Noise predominates in all parts of the house. Her mother, sister, and one slovenly servant keep the household running in a somewhat competent manner, though without any of the polish or precision that she is used to at Mansfield Park. Her father is rarely home, spending most of his time drinking, and when he is at home, his presence only makes Fanny more uncomfortable. Nowhere can Fanny find a place where she can enjoy the peace, privacy, and tranquillity she is used to. She has found herself in the midst of a lower-class household with neither the manners nor the sensibilities of her Mansfield relatives.

Sir Thomas's plan to make Fanny appreciate Mansfield Park and Henry Crawford more in light of her birth family's lifestyle is successful. What Sir Thomas perceives of as ingratitude towards him and his family is not really ingratitude, but Fanny's understanding of precisely what she is grateful for does become much clearer while she is in Portsmouth. She misses her Mansfield companions intensely, and when Henry Crawford comes to Portsmouth to visit her, she is grateful and excited to be able to talk with someone who knows the people she knows and who shares the lifestyle to which she has been accustomed. Henry continues his attempt to make Fanny fall in love with him and agree to marry him, and in such a setting as Portsmouth, his demeanor and even his character seem more acceptable to Fanny. She continues to believe that she can never marry him, but his aristocratic manners together with his knowledge of those dearest to her makes him a companion to whom it is hard to say goodbye. Nonetheless, Henry leaves, planning to visit Mary in London.

Meanwhile, trouble is brewing in the Bertram family. Tom, the eldest son and heir to the family fortune, falls ill with a life-threatening fever. He had been carousing with his friends in Newmarket, when he experienced a rather serious fall from his horse. That fall, combined with an overindulgence of drunkenness with his friends, had resulted in a fever. Tom is brought home to Mansfield

Park to recover, but for some time his life hangs in the balance. He eventually recovers and, as a result of his bout with fever, determines that he must, in future, act with greater responsibility and morality.

But Tom has not yet fully recovered when the next blow falls. Still in Portsmouth, Fanny receives the news that her cousin Maria has run off with Henry Crawford. The two of them became reacquainted in London, and after a rather public flirtation, they disappeared together. Mr. Rushworth, publicly humiliated, threw off his wife completely, and Sir Thomas was put in the position of having to find his daughter and bring her back to Mansfield in disgrace. He refuses, however, to have her under his own roof and instead arranges with his sister-in-law, Mrs. Norris, to live with her far from Mansfield.

The third blow follows when Julia elopes to Scotland with John Yates. Sir Thomas then sends for Fanny to return to Mansfield Park to comfort Lady Bertram. And so Fanny returns to Mansfield to be with those she loves best.

Fanny believes that Edmund must, based on Henry's behavior with Maria, have given up all hope of a future marriage to Mary Crawford. She waits, however, to hear from him exactly how things stand between them. Edmund still loves Mary, but he now sees her true character. Mary considers the behavior of her brother and Maria to be "folly," nothing more (Vol. II, 285). She suggests that they ease the scandal by convincing Henry to marry Maria. "[W]hen once married," she explains, "and properly supported by her own family . . . she may recover her footing in society to a certain degree" (Vol. II, 289). Edmund finally realizes that Mary is not the morally superior person he has tried to convince himself she is. Whereas he could attribute her earlier slips in propriety to an improper upbringing, this explicit illustration of her lack of basic moral values convinces him that he could never marry her. He continues to love her, but he can no longer respect her.

As Fanny and Edmund console each other and the other members of the family, they become even closer than before. Without the charming distraction of Mary Crawford, Edmund comes to recognize how much he and Fanny have in common and how much he has come to depend upon her, even to love her. Years before, when first considering whether to take Fanny into his household or not, Sir Thomas had been momentarily concerned that a relationship might form between his niece and one of his sons, an occurrence he was determined to prevent. But at this point in their lives, he is "[s]ick of ambitious and mercenary connections" and he prizes "more and more the sterling good of principle and temper" that Fanny represents (Vol. II, 308). Edmund Bertram finally marries Fanny Price, and together they serve the needs of Edmund's family and his parishes as representatives of moral rectitude in a society that often seems to be lacking that quality.

CHARACTER DEVELOPMENT

In *Mansfield Park*, the most important quality in each character is his or her fundamental morality. In an England that was suffering from the moral weaknesses of many among the royalty and aristocracy, the subject of how true morality is defined and identified through actions was of considerable consequence to the population as a whole. In *Mansfield Park*, Jane Austen created a fictional world which examines absolute morality vs. situational ethics.

Fanny Price is the character who most fully represents moral absolutism. She believes that right and wrong are clearly defined concepts and that one should always adhere to what is right, regardless of the pressure one receives from loved ones or from the world at large. Fanny operates at all times from a clear understanding of propriety. She recognizes her obligations to her aunts and uncle, and always attempts to fulfill those obligations fully. However, when pressured by her uncle to marry a man she does not love, a man whom she knows to have behaved dishonorably towards her family in the past, she does not give in to pressure. She knows that her obligations towards those who have raised her do not require her to marry without love or respect for her mate. Thus, even though Sir Thomas's accusations of ingratitude hurt her deeply, her understanding of morality as absolute prevents her from accepting his judgment of her when she rejects Henry Crawford's proposal of marriage.

Fanny's sense of propriety also prevents her from assuming that she should have the same rights and privileges as the cousins with whom she is raised. Fanny understands from a very early age that her position in the family is one of a dependent relative. Her cousins Maria and Julia treat her as an outsider, as little more than a servant, but she never complains, nor does she seem even to resent such behavior. She willingly performs errands for her Aunt Norris, even when running those errands at times damages her health. When her cousins go visiting, she is often expected to remain behind to keep her Aunt Bertram company. Fanny never complains. She accepts these expectations as a means by which she can show her gratitude to her aunts and uncle for all they have given her.

The cousin who comes closest to Fanny in his display of morality is Edmund Bertram. He, like Fanny, has learned early in life to accept that he will not be the favored one. As the younger brother, he is expected to be able to make his own way in the world while his elder brother, Tom, inherits the estate and all the income accruing to it. Our more democratic twenty-first century sensibilities may consider such a distribution of family wealth to be unjustifiable, but Edmund, like most younger sons of wealthy families in Austen's time, simply accepts it as the way things are.

Edmund begins the novel with an absolute morality like Fanny, but he is swayed towards situational ethics when his siblings and friends decide to mount a play. Edmund, like Fanny, believes such an enterprise is wrong. The choices of plays they consider are inappropriate, requiring that impressionable young people act the parts of lovers with one another. And, if that were not sufficient, Edmund knows that his father heartily disapproves of family theatricals. Nonetheless, despite Edmund's awareness that presenting such a play is wrong, he allows himself to be persuaded to participate. His participation would, he rationalizes, enable him to be on the inside, where he may be able to use his influence to keep the size of the audience and the elaboration of the set design to a minimum. In addition, he rationalizes, his participation will prevent Mary Crawford from having to act the part of a lover with a complete stranger.

Tom Bertram behaves, throughout most of the novel, as a rather typical fashionable eldest son. He is raised knowing that he will never have to work for a living: his only job will be to control and maintain the vast holdings and income that his father holds before him. His definition of morality can best be described as personal gratification: what he wants is right, and anything that gets in his way is wrong. When Sir Thomas reprimands Tom for having contracted extensive gambling debts which require the sale of a clerical position that he has been holding for his younger son, Edmund, Tom

listened with some shame and some sorrow; but escaping as quickly as possible, could soon with cheerful selfishness reflect, 1st, that he had not been half so much in debt as some of his friends; 2dly, that his father had made a most tiresome piece of work of it; and 3dly, that the future incumbent [the clergyman who bought the clerical position Sir Thomas sold], whoever he might be, would, in all probability, die very soon. (Vol. I, 32)

Tom's view of morality is entirely subjective. He expects the world to operate according to his desires and does not care whether his actions impact others negatively.

The Bertram daughters, like their elder brother, operate from a situational ethics perspective. Maria, as the elder and more pampered daughter, expects to take precedence over her sister Julia, her cousin Fanny, and almost any other woman in company with them. She, with her Aunt Norris's assistance, engages the attention and heart of Mr. Rushworth, a rather simple-minded gentleman who has inherited the grand estate of Sotherton. Maria never even imagines that she feels any love for Mr. Rushworth. Her goal is to marry into an estate, to become the hostess of that estate as well as a London house, and to participate in society at the highest levels. With Mr. Rushworth as a husband, she can achieve that goal.

When Henry Crawford enters the picture, however, Maria's situation becomes complicated. Suddenly a fascinating, charming, and handsome young man with a fortune of his own is flirting with her. She is attracted to him and would rather create a future life with him than with Mr. Rushworth. On the other hand, Mr. Rushworth and his estate, Sotherton, are guaranteed whereas Henry Crawford has made no commitment. Maria wants to keep both men, if possible. She flirts outrageously with Henry while maintaining her plans to marry Rushworth. When Henry leaves the neighborhood, making it clear that he has no intention of marrying her, she hastily marries her fiancé, only to be tempted into a flirtation and a plan to run away with Henry Crawford before she has even completed her wedding trip. Maria, like her older brother Tom, acts out of pure selfishness and a sense of entitlement.

The Crawford siblings are more attractive constructions of Tom and Maria Bertram, with a twist. Their personalities are much more appealing, and their upbringing seems to have provided them with a legitimate excuse for some of their lapses in proper behavior, but essentially they both operate under the principle: what I want is what is right, *providing* I keep up appearances. Mary and Henry Crawford were raised by their uncle and aunt, Admiral and Mrs. Crawford. The elder Crawfords' marriage was very unhappy, which influenced their niece and nephew's beliefs about relationships tremendously. Many of the younger Crawfords' views about life were colored by their aunt and uncle's experience. Thus, when Mary Crawford makes comments about marriage and the clergy that Edmund considers improper, he attributes the ideas behind those comments to the influence of her aunt and uncle. He assumes that, with the right influences, she would rapidly learn to hold sounder values that match his own.

By the end of the novel, however, even Edmund is forced to admit that Mary does not operate according to the standards of morality that he and Fanny believe in. To Mary, Maria's leaving a wealthy husband, a grand estate, and an assurance of an active social life for a temporary fling with her brother is foolish, not reprehensible. Such a slip could, she believes, be covered over and life would continue as before. For Mary, right and wrong are not in the doing but in whether anyone else is aware of what one has done and whether those who are aware are willing to overlook it. Hide the evidence, act as though nothing is wrong, and most of society, Mary believes, will pretend along with you.

Henry Crawford, like Tom Bertram, is an eldest son. His parents having died when he was very young, he has already inherited his estate by the time the novel opens. He has been raised to a life of privilege and expects others to defer to him. His position in life, like Tom's, has not forced him to consider the feelings of others, and his upbringing with his uncle, Admiral Crawford, operated as a means of increasing Henry's selfishness and his belief that he should not have to face any negative consequences for his actions.

Henry's one chance to develop a strong moral center comes after the Bertram sisters have left home when he decides to make Fanny fall in love with him. His intentions at the outset of this experiment are cold and noncommittal, but in Fanny he finds a formidable challenge. As he comes to know her, he learns that his own behavior will have to change if he is to have even the slightest chance of conquest. And as his admiration for her grows, his intentions change. Fanny, he decides, is a woman with whom he could spend a lifetime. No longer does he want merely to gain a piece of her heart; instead he wants her, body and soul, to be his wife. At this point in Henry's development, it seems possible that he really has learned his lesson and that he will be able to become a morally upright man with whom Fanny can build a happy and productive future.

Many of Austen's readers through the years (including her own sister, Cassandra), have felt that Henry's change of heart is sufficient to make him the moral creature that Fanny needs as a husband. Austen herself apparently disagreed. Instead, she allows Henry to revert to his more typical behavior. Unable to resist the urge to flirt once again with Maria Rushworth, despite his protestation that he is in love with Fanny and disregarding the fact that Maria is married and still on her honeymoon trip, Henry falls from grace. He wins Maria, a woman he does not even want, away from her husband and, in the process, loses any chance he ever had of marrying Fanny. Loving a good woman, one may infer, is not sufficient motivation to overturn a lifetime of acting selfishly. Had Fanny married Henry, it is unlikely that his love for her would have kept him on the proper moral path for long. Henry's basic sense of morality has not changed. He wants Fanny and thinks he is willing to do whatever it takes to win her. When presented with the temptation of seducing Maria, however, even his attempt to live a more ethical life in order to win Fanny does not enable him to resist years of training in selfishness and disregard for the feelings of others.

THEMATIC ISSUES

In *Mansfield Park*, as in most of Jane Austen's fiction, one's social status influences almost everything in one's life. Every detail of one's birth (and for women, marriage)—from the level of society to which one's family belongs to whether one is born male or female, eldest or youngest within a family—works together to determine one's place in the hierarchy of family, community, and even nation in Austen's England. *Mansfield Park* illustrates the gradations of social status within families best of all of Austen's novels. Throughout the novel,

Austen explores the theme of how one's social position within the family affects the development of character.

Mansfield Park functions as a microcosm of England. Sir Thomas, owner of the estate and holder of immense wealth, is the leader. His demands are always met. No one challenges him openly, although his children do, at times, go against his wishes when he is not around. Fanny's refusal to marry Henry Crawford is the closest thing to a real challenge Sir Thomas faces. But according to tradition, Fanny has the right of refusal in matrimony, and she exercises that right despite Sir Thomas's displeasure.

Lady Bertram is an insubstantial and ineffective woman who enjoys the luxuries of life as the wife of a baronet without having to take responsibility for anything. As the wife of a wealthy landowner, she has no need to be useful unless she chooses. Since she is content sitting on her sofa, she does not attempt anything more. According to the law of the land in Austen's time, a woman loses her individual and independent identity when she is married. She and her husband become one entity in the eyes of the law, and that entity is the husband (See Chapter 3 for further discussion of coverture). In the marriage of Sir Thomas and Lady Bertram, the law of coverture is played out. There is only one active force in the marriage, and that force is Sir Thomas. Lady Bertram is so passive as to seem almost invisible, the embodiment of *feme covert*, the hidden or invisible woman under law.

Mrs. Norris is nothing like her sister, the baronet's wife. In fact, of the two members of the Norris couple, the reader meets only the wife. That Mrs. Norris is an active force in the novel is appropriate to her social position. Clergymen of the lower gentry level of society in late eighteenth-century England tended to have sufficient money to keep the rectory in good operating condition and to support a small family, but unless he had also inherited substantial wealth, he rarely had extra for luxuries. Many clergymen's wives helped out by running a family dairy and small farm or garden. A clergyman's wife also often took charge of many of the benevolent activities in the community and, if the local landowning family was not in residence in the community, she and her husband often directed much of the community's social life. Mrs. Norris has no children of her own to take care of, feed, and support, so her spending her time and energy taking care of a family farm or dairy is unnecessary. Because Sir Thomas is in residence at Mansfield Park, Mrs. Norris and her husband do not have the obligation of directing the social activities of the community or to be the primary benefactors of those in need. But Mrs. Norris does have the energy and desire to make herself useful and important in her community. As a result, she often takes on responsibilities that might more reasonably be handled by her sister, Lady Bertram, were Lady Bertram's personality a more active one. She spends much of her time in the Bertram household supervising her nieces' education, suggesting appropriate benevolent activities to Sir Thomas, even making Maria's wedding plans. Mrs. Norris is active, as a clergyman's wife should be. Her activity is not always productive of good, but the activity itself suits her status in society.

The third sister, Mrs. Price, finds herself in need of the energy that Mrs. Norris has. As the mother of nine children living in working-class accommodations in a port town, Mrs. Price has no time or energy to do anything other than take care of her home, her husband, and her children. She never even leaves her home except on Sundays when she goes to church and takes a quick walk along the wharf before beginning the next week's work. Mrs. Price is active from early morning to late night providing the basic necessities for her family. Such was the situation for most women of the working classes in Austen's England.

Among the younger generation at Mansfield Park, Tom represents that portion of the generation who is destined to inherit the wealth of England. Just as the Royal Princes of England enjoy a carefree lifestyle in which they obey few rules and show respect for even fewer, so does Tom Bertram refuse to live by the rules of propriety and decorum that his father expects him to follow. Instead, Tom rules over the house in his father's absence, almost as though he already owns it. He excuses himself for his gambling debts by reminding himself that many of his friends are even further in debt. He encourages his siblings and friends to put on an unsuitable play at a time when putting together any theatrical performance, let alone the one they choose, is inappropriate. Tom Bertram, like so many of his generation, expects to enjoy the privileges of his social status without having to accept responsibility. If the family is fortunate, Tom's bout with a life-threatening illness combined with his father's attempts to train him as a businessman will enable Tom to grow into a responsible and caring landowner. What the future will hold for Tom continues to be questionable at the end of the novel, however, just as the future of England under the rule of the Prince Regent seemed uncertain to many of Austen's contemporaries.

Maria and Julia Bertram hold very similar positions in the society of which Mansfield Park is a part. Both are daughters of a wealthy and well-respected landowner. Both have expectations of marrying wealthy men and becoming mistresses over lavish estates. And both, as women of the landed classes, have no lifestyle options beyond marriage or life as a dependent sister or aunt. One subtle, though important, difference exists, however, between the social status of Maria and Julia, and that difference dictates how each woman ultimately behaves. As the firstborn female, Maria takes precedence over Julia throughout their childhood and premarriage years. Until she marries, Maria will always be "Miss Ward" and Julia "Miss Julia Ward." Such a distinction may seem trite today, but in Austen's time it was significant. Eldest daughters led the way in society: they were given the more desirable seats at dinner parties; they led the way at dances and parties; they received the first invitations; they were introduced before their younger sisters. Maria Bertram was raised as a young girl used to getting her way in everything. Julia, on the other hand, understood from a very early age that she must always give way to her sister.

But if Julia must give way to Maria, Fanny, in her position as the dependent cousin who has been saved from a life of poverty by the goodness of her uncle's heart, must give way to *everyone* in the household. Fanny's status at Mansfield Park is little better than a servant's. She sleeps in the attic and, once her cousins' schooldays are over, is allowed only the unheated schoolroom to use for private study and activity. Fanny is expected to show gratitude to her benefactors at all times. She must give way to her cousins' desires over her own. She must be willing to keep Lady Bertram company and run errands for Mrs. Norris with never a complaint. Such is the life of a dependent female relative in Jane Austen's England.

Fanny is fortunate in many ways. She receives an excellent education for a girl of her time, something she could not have acquired had she remained at Portsmouth with her parents. She is introduced into society. Perhaps most important for her future happiness, she is raised as befits the wife of a gentleman clergyman. Being raised at Mansfield Park prepares her well for the role of wife to the future clergyman, Edmund Bertram.

Edmund, as the younger son in the Bertram family, has more in common with Fanny than with any of his siblings. While they are being raised with the expectations of being taken care of for life (Tom by his inheritance of Mansfield Park, his sisters by marriage to wealthy men), Edmund is raised knowing that he will have to support himself. Therefore Edmund, like Fanny, has to consider a less affluent adulthood than his childhood might otherwise lead him to expect. As a younger son choosing a profession among the clergy, Edmund will retain his status as a gentleman, but he will move from his birth status to that of lower gentry as soon as he enters into his profession.

Social status in the England of Austen's time determined much about a person's upbringing, expectations, and possibilities. The social status of the characters at Mansfield Park itself is stable, representing the way things have been for generations. One character in the novel, however, represents a future in which social status can be earned by merit as well as birth. William Price, Fanny's beloved brother, joins the Navy. There, through a combination of hard work and the influence of powerful people, he has the opportunity, if he handles himself well, to create a life for himself that is not predetermined by his birth. William starts his rise in status within the novel; he has not yet fulfilled his potential by its close. The focus on William's successes, however, indicates the likelihood that he can achieve more than the son of his father might have expected. In the novel, *Persuasion*, Austen returns to the subject of a young man raising himself socially and materially through his own efforts in the Navy. In *Mansfield Park* that possibility is only hinted at in the character of William Price.

A PSYCHOLOGICAL READING OF THE CHARACTER OF FANNY PRICE

In the twentieth century, the development of the study of psychology has provided readers of literature with invaluable tools for the exploration of character, especially in the novel. The novel by its very nature is structured to illuminate the way individuals function within a community and, as an extension of that community, in society at large. Writers of realistic novels must, therefore, in order to successfully depict that interaction, provide their characters with realistic motivations. By examining characters psychologically, therefore, the reader can come to a greater understanding of both the individual characters and the society in which they participate.

Jane Austen takes great care to present most of her characters in as psychologically realistic a manner as possible. By examining a character's behavior, a reader can, with some knowledge of the culture of Austen's England, construct a logical background that would be likely to develop such behavior. Likewise, knowledge of the background of a character can provide that reader with a fairly accurate expectation of how a character will act in a given situation. In *Mansfield Park*, Austen is particularly careful to provide her readers with the environmental and family background of most of her characters as well as to describe in considerable detail the actions characters take and the motivations behind them.

In the character of Fanny Price, Austen creates a young girl with a confusing and difficult childhood. Until the age of nine, she resides with her birth family, which includes a mother who dotes on her sons but has no use for girls, a father who is often drunk and can barely provide for the family's most basic needs, and several siblings. Among those siblings, only one treats her with care and respect, her brother William. Such a life could not have provided the young girl with a healthy sense of self-esteem. At the age of nine, she learns that she will be moving far from the only home she has ever known to live with relatives she has never met. She travels from the rough town of Portsmouth to Mansfield Park, a grand estate in the country. There she meets her relatives: Sir Thomas, a rather intimidating and seemingly cold gentleman; Lady Bertram, a quiet, self-involved woman who rarely rises from her sofa; Mrs. Norris, a cold, demanding woman who treats Fanny as though she is little better than a servant; and her cousins, four young people who have never known a moment's true deprivation in their lives.

Although the change in environment is good for Fanny's health and will provide her with advantages she could never have had in Portsmouth, it is still a traumatic change. Such a change creates tremendous stress on a person, even more so when that person is a young child who does not understand the reasons for it. Thus Fanny cannot help but be insecure in her new environment. She knows what life was like for her at Portsmouth, and she knows that she could, at any time, be returned to her birth family. Over time her memories of Portsmouth dim, but her insecurity remains.

During her years at Mansfield Park, only one of her four cousins treats her well. To Tom, Maria, and Julia, Fanny is merely another body in the house, but to Edmund, Fanny is someone to befriend. He is the one individual in the entire household who treats her like a human being, with likes and dislikes, with needs and desires. Even Sir Thomas, who does genuinely care for his niece and wants the best for her, never checks to see that her needs are met. Instead, he assumes that others in the household are looking after her adequately.

In Edmund, Fanny recreates the closeness she felt with her brother William, the only one of her siblings who cares deeply for her. The fact that Edmund is not her brother, however, complicates those feelings. She is raised in his childhood home along with his sisters, but the distinction made between her and them at every turn reinforces the fact that she is *not* his sister. As a result, Fanny's feelings for her cousin grow deeper and deeper, evolving into a love that can only be satisfied in marriage.

When Fanny is seventeen or eighteen, her life once again takes an abrupt turn when her uncle, displeased that she has rejected a marriage proposal he believes she should accept, sends her to her parents in Portsmouth for a visit. While a visit to her parents does not sound like an unreasonable event in a young woman's life, Fanny is well aware that she is leaving Mansfield Park under the cloud of Sir Thomas's disapproval, and although she knows that her trip to Portsmouth is intended to be a visit, not permanent exile, her childhood insecurities would undoubtedly resurface as she left Mansfield, especially since the date of her return remained unscheduled.

Fanny's visit to Portsmouth seems interminable to her. She no longer has a designated position in the family of her birth, and she desperately misses the family at Mansfield Park. Fanny expects to be at Portsmouth only a few weeks, but weeks stretch into months. Only after a three-month absence is she allowed to return.

If Fanny has any doubts about her reception back into the Mansfield fold, they do not last long. Sir Thomas welcomes her back with tremendous affection. Lady Bertram is delighted to have her return, having missed her company more than that of either of her two daughters, both of whom have been away from home longer than Fanny. Mrs. Norris is harsh, blaming Fanny for Maria's difficulties by refusing to marry Henry Crawford, but Mrs. Norris is not around long enough to cause Fanny serious discomfort. If any insecurities about her place in the Bertram family remain after this warm homecoming, they must surely be resolved once Edmund, having overcome his long-held infatuation with Mary Crawford, asks for and receives Fanny's hand in marriage.

Fanny is perfectly suited, by both temperament and upbringing, to be a country clergyman's wife. She is used to being of service to her aunts; thus she will find being of service to those in her husband's parish a satisfying experience. Her experiences of deprivation with her family in Portsmouth as well as those of luxury and comfort with her Mansfield Park family will enable her to understand the lives and the points of view of people from many walks of life. Her skills in household economy will make her a careful and economical housekeeper for a clergyman with a limited income. But most of all, her sense of morality as an absolute standard will enable her to assist her husband in his parish work, which includes being the arbiter of any moral controversy in his community. In Fanny, Austen has given her readers a realistic depiction of the psychological development of a woman who endures much and becomes the best person she can become both because of and in spite of that endurance.

6

Emma
(1815)

In 1813, Jane Austen was a successful author with two popular novels in print and a third ready to go to press. Her confidence and her creativity were at an all-time high, and she was thrilled over the fact that she had money of her own, money for which she did not have to thank her brothers or friends.

The identity of the author of *Sense and Sensibility* and *Pride and Prejudice*, while still officially a secret, became a much less guarded secret during the writing of *Emma*. Henry Austen, the novelist's brother, acted as her agent with the London publishers. His pride in his famous sister often overwhelmed his sense of discretion, and he frequently revealed her identity against her wishes. Among those who learned of the author's identity through Henry's indiscretions was the Prince Regent, whose doctor was also Henry Austen's doctor. He had learned from Henry that Jane was not only the author but that she was, at that time, in London visiting him. The Prince Regent, upon hearing that the author of such celebrated works was in London, ordered his librarian, James Stanier Clarke, to call on her, to invite her to his library at Carlton House, and to suggest that she dedicate her next book to him. Austen detested the behavior of the Prince Regent who lived quite openly with his mistress and made the life of his wife quite miserable. *Mansfield Park*, the novel previous to *Emma*, made clear her feelings about the detestable nature of adultery and unfaithfulness in any form. Yet she realized that a suggestion from the Prince Regent's librarian was essentially a Royal order. So, *Emma* was published with a dedication to His Royal Highness, the Prince Regent, as distasteful as it was to Austen to do so.

While *Mansfield Park* is often considered to be Austen's problem novel, scholars often refer to *Emma* as her perfect novel. Austen biographer Claire Tomalin writes that "*Emma*, with its far from faultless heroine, is generally hailed as Austen's most perfect book, flawlessly carried out from conception to finish, without a rough patch or a loose end" (248). The plotting is strong throughout, and the characters are painted with a very fine brush. As a result, most readers are captivated by the novel about a young woman determined to control the lives of those around her, despite her immaturity and inability to discern what is really best for people, including herself. In *Emma*, Austen writes for the first time from the perspective of a young woman who was born to wealth and power. Emma Woodhouse is not a member of the aristocracy with a vast fortune, but she is definitely the wealthiest woman in her part of the countryside of England. She always takes precedence in her social circle and is looked to by others in her community as the leader of local society. Such a woman is far removed from Fanny Price; even the Dashwood and Bennet girls could have no understanding of what it is like for a woman like Emma to grow up knowing that she need never worry about the possibility of being impoverished. By creating such a character, Austen allowed herself to imagine what the mind of a young woman might become if it did not have to be concerned constantly with the expenses of everyday life.

PLOT DEVELOPMENT

Emma opens with a description of the main character, Emma Woodhouse, who is "handsome, clever, and rich" and who, "with a comfortable home and happy disposition, seemed to unite some of the best blessings of existence; and had lived nearly twenty-one years in the world with very little to distress her" (1). We are told that she is the younger of two daughters, that her father is "most affectionate" and "indulgent," and that she has "been mistress of [her father's] house from a very early period" due to her mother's death and her sister's marriage (1). Emma is, therefore, quite different from any of Austen's earlier fictional heroines. She has no obstacles of poverty or social position to overcome. She does not even need to concern herself with finding a husband unless she chooses to do so since, unlike the Bennet estate in *Pride and Prejudice*, there is no entailment on her father's estate that would cause it to be inherited away from her and she has no brother to inherit the property through the rule of primogeniture. Emma is free to live her life very much as she chooses.

The plot of *Emma*, like that of *Sense and Sensibility* and *Pride and Prejudice*, centers on courtship, but the focus is very different in this novel than in Austen's earlier ones. In *Emma*, the focus is on Emma's activity of choice: matchmaking. By observing Emma as she actively attempts to match the men and women of her community, the reader can watch Emma develop from an adolescent girl who wrongly believes she knows what is best for everyone around her into a young woman who gradually gains the discernment necessary to be a morally upright and caring young woman fit to be mistress of a vast estate and wife to an exceptional and benevolent gentleman.

The novel opens with reference to a wedding. Miss Taylor, Emma's former governess, has recently been married to Mr. Weston, a former military man who now owns property near Highbury. Emma feels a certain amount of sadness about the wedding, understanding that Miss Taylor will never again be living with her at Hartfield, and that she will never again have the place of highest importance in her former governess's heart, a position she does not give up easily. She is grateful, however, that, as Mrs. Weston, her dear friend will remain in the neighborhood where they can visit frequently. Despite the fact that Emma actually had very little to do with Mr. Weston falling in love with Miss Taylor, she takes a certain amount of pride in what she considers to have been her part in matching the couple with each other. The match of Mr. and Mrs. Weston is, she believes, her first successful act of matchmaking.

The Woodhouses of Hartfield are the family of highest social standing in the neighborhood of Highbury, but one other family is of equal social status: the Knightley family who owns the property of Donwell Abbey, the estate that adjoins Hartfield. John Knightley, the younger of two sons, is married to Emma's sister, Isabella. They and their children live in London where John practices law. His elder brother George, "a sensible man, about seven or eight-and-thirty," lives at Donwell Abbey, supervising the farm and acting as landlord for those who live and work on his property (5). He also assists Mr. Woodhouse with the operation of his estate, since Mr. Woodhouse suffers from hypochondria and is, as a result, unable to care for his estate as thoroughly as is expected of a man in his position.

After Miss Taylor marries Mr. Weston, Emma is left on her own to find a new friend to become her daily companion. She chooses Harriet Smith, a young woman from the local girls' boarding school. Harriet is a sweet and gentle young woman who lives at the school full time. She does not know who her parents are, and most people assume that, since her tuition and board at Mrs. Goddard's school are paid regularly, she must be the "natural" (illegitimate) child of a man of property.

Emma sets out to befriend Harriet, certain that she can greatly assist a young woman who has been raised to be genteel but has no known family. Emma decides to help Harriet find an appropriate husband, someone who holds a social position that will keep Harriet in Emma's social circle even after she is married. The unmarried gentleman she decides is the best fit for Harriet is Mr. Elton, the rector of Highbury.

Harriet is thrilled to have Emma show such an interest in her. She is a very simple young woman who greatly admires Emma Woodhouse and who is ready to believe that Emma's position in society gives her greater wisdom than Harriet herself can ever have—even about her own life. Therefore, Harriet is willing to take Emma's opinion as her own on most subjects.

Early in the novel, Harriet is flattered by the attentions of a local farmer, Robert Martin. Robert is known to be a fine young man. He works hard, supporting his widowed mother and two sisters through his labor. Harriet has known Robert Martin for many years through his sisters who have been among her closest friends at Mrs. Goddard's school. When Robert seems to be on the verge of asking her to marry him, Harriet is thrilled. She runs to Emma, excited to share the information with her new friend. Emma, however, does not react as Harriet expects. In fact, Emma is horrified that Harriet would even consider attaching herself to a man of such low social standing as Robert Martin. Such a marriage, Emma tells Harriet, would lower her social position to the point at which she and Harriet would no longer be able to be friends. She tells Harriet that she must end all interaction with the Martin family if she wants to maintain her relationship with Hartfield and the Woodhouses. Harriet, believing her friend to be the better judge of what is proper, breaks off her connection with the Martins, even though such a break makes her extremely uncomfortable.

Emma is pleased with Harriet for ending her relationship with the Martin family, and she immediately sets to work on the match between Mr. Elton and Harriet. She arranges social occasions in such a way that Harriet and Mr. Elton will be thrown together frequently. She encourages Mr. Elton to come by Hartfield to visit when Harriet is around. She sets up situations, such as a game of conundrums, which Mr. Elton can use as a means of communicating his interest in courting Harriet. And Mr. Elton seems to swallow the bait. He contributes a conundrum for the word "courtship" to their game, a contribution that Emma interprets as an indirect flirtation with her protégé. He overly admires a drawing of Harriet that Emma has made, which Emma interprets as his admiration for the subject of the drawing.

Emma is wrong, however, in her assumption that Mr. Elton is interested in Harriet. Her error becomes vividly apparent to her one night when she and Mr. Elton share a carriage on the way home from a party at the Weston's. Harriet is absent from the party because of a bad cold. As Emma and Mr. Elton talk, Emma continues to try to direct the conversation towards the subject of Harriet. Mr. Elton, however, does not cooperate. In fact, as becomes clear even to Emma, Mr. Elton is on the verge of proposing marriage to Emma Woodhouse, not Harriet Smith. Emma is stunned. She cannot imagine how Mr. Elton can believe that she would ever consider him to be good enough to marry someone with her family background and social standing. Mr. Elton explains that her behavior towards him has encouraged him to believe that she wanted him to be interested in her. He describes the very events which she orchestrated to interest him in Harriet and explains how he interpreted them as indications of Emma's interest in him. Mr. Elton is highly insulted that Emma would think Harriet, a woman who is probably of illegitimate birth, could be a suitable mate for him. The evening ends with a permanent cessation of any real intimacy between Mr. Elton and the Woodhouse family.

Emma is then left with the task of telling Harriet that Mr. Elton is not, in fact, interested in her as anything other than Emma's friend. Harriet is, of course, disappointed. She has so trusted Emma's interpretation of events that she has allowed herself to hope for a future as Mrs. Elton. Emma decides to give Harriet time for her emotions to recover before attempting another, hopefully more successful, matchmaking effort for her young friend.

Meanwhile, Emma finds herself to be the subject of some matchmaking on the part of her former governess and her husband. Mr. Weston has a son by his first marriage who is of an appropriate age to court Emma. That son, Frank Churchill, lives with his late mother's parents as their heir. His taking of the Churchill name is a result of that situation. Frank has been rumored to be planning a visit to his father on and off for years, but each scheduled visit, for one reason or another, has been cancelled, usually at the last moment. At this point in the story, however, Frank's plans to visit seem to be set. Since his father has just remarried, most of the people at Highbury believe that Frank could not possibly cancel this visit. Anything less than an immediate visit in his father's home would be a direct insult to his father and, most especially, to his father's new bride.

Mrs. Weston expects that Frank, upon meeting Emma, will choose to court her as his future wife. She lets Emma know of this expectation. Emma, while professing vigorously that she does not expect ever to marry, is intrigued by the idea of being courted by the attractive and worldly young gentleman. When Frank finally arrives for his long-promised visit, Emma finds spending time with him quite agreeable. She enjoys mutual flirtation with him, though she never seriously considers a future with him.

Shortly before Frank's arrival in Highbury, an attractive young woman arrives in town. Jane Fairfax, the granddaughter of the former vicar in Highbury, comes home to stay with her grandmother after completing her education with her good friend, Miss Campbell. Miss Campbell's father had been in the military with Jane's father, and when Jane's parents died, Mr. Campbell provided for the young orphan. He raised her with his daughter, providing her with an education fit for a gentlewoman, thus saving her impoverished grandmother from having an additional financial burden thrust upon her. As a result, Jane

Fairfax has a background appropriate for a lady. With such a background she could, if she found a man who did not care whether his wife had financial resources of her own, marry into the landed classes. If such a marriage did not present itself, she would be highly qualified to earn her living as a governess or a teacher in a school for girls.

Jane's coming to Highbury coincides with Miss Campbell's getting married and going to Ireland on her wedding trip. At that point, despite the fact that the Campbells have told her she can stay with them as long as she chooses, Jane decides to remove the burden of her care from the Campbell family. Her visit with her grandmother and aunt is to be a transitional step before finding herself a means of support for the future.

Emma, with her mind constantly on matchmaking, comes up with a more complicated explanation for Jane's having left the Campbells. Her romantic sensibility suggests that Jane may have been in love with Mr. Dixon, the new husband of her best friend. The feelings, she suspects, are mutual: Mr. Dixon is also in love with the beautiful Jane Fairfax. But Mr. Dixon, needing to marry a woman of means, married Miss Campbell and left Jane Fairfax to suffer in silence.

Emma shares her suspicions about Jane's love life with Frank Churchill, who encourages her in them. The interaction between Emma and Frank regarding Jane clearly makes the poor young woman very uncomfortable, but that doesn't stop Frank from making relatively public insinuations. When a piano arrives in Highbury as a gift for Jane, most people in the community assume that the Campbells have sent it. Frank, however, suggests that it is a gift from Mr. Dixon, a gift expressing his continuing affection for her even after his marriage to her friend. When asked about the piano, Jane becomes disconcerted, lending credibility to the possibility that the piano is not a gift from the Campbells, but instead a tribute from a secret lover.

Jane's future becomes a subject of concern to a number of people in town. Several offer their assistance in helping Jane find suitable employment as a governess or teacher, but Jane insists that she can find employment for herself when the time is right. Late in the novel, due to some behind-the-scenes action the reader is unaware of at the time, Jane finally decides to accept a position as governess and makes the arrangements necessary to begin her life as an independent woman. When Frank Churchill finds out what she has done, the real story of her leaving the Campbells and visiting Highbury finally comes out. Jane and Frank had, in fact, met while she was still living with the Campbells. They had fallen in love and had secretly engaged themselves to be married. The engagement had to remain secret, however, since Frank was still dependent on his grandparents who expected a different kind of marriage for him.

Frank's visit to his father in Highbury came about primarily, therefore, because it allowed him to be near the woman he loved. He and Jane could meet secretly in Highbury and the surrounding countryside. Although Frank did appreciate his father's new wife, his visit to Highbury may very well have been postponed yet again had he not had the presence of his fiancée to draw him there.

Frank's teasing with Emma about Jane's secret love for Mr. Dixon was, therefore, a good cover for his own interest in her as well as a joke on Emma. The infamous piano that made Jane so uncomfortable was a gift from Frank, not the Campbells or Mr. Dixon, and the speculation it raised as to where it had come from had given Jane much uneasiness. Jane was also discomfitted by the relationship developing between her fiancé and Emma Woodhouse. Almost everyone in town seemed to assume that Frank and Emma were destined for marriage, and seeing them together so publicly when she was forced to pretend in company that she and Frank were nothing to each other, made her doubt Frank's commitment to her.

Jane's hesitance to trust Frank's commitment to marry her led her, finally, to accept a position as governess. She knows that she must find a way to provide for her future. If Frank Churchill is not committed to take care of her through marriage, then she must find a way to provide for herself. Jane has no desire to be a governess, but she sees no other respectable alternative. Only when Frank discovers Jane's intentions does he realize he has gone too far. He then hurries to Jane and makes amends to her for his inconsiderate behavior.

Mrs. Weston is placed in the position of having to tell Emma that Frank is not available and has, in fact, been leading her on. Emma is surprised by the news, but assures her friend that she is not really disappointed. She has not become nearly as attached to Frank as the community has believed. She acknowledges that Frank was wrong to lead her on as he did, but the damage done by his irresponsible flirtation is negligible as far as her heart is concerned.

Emma's heart is safe from Frank's flirtations because she already has attached herself to another man, though she remains unaware of any such attachment at a conscious level. Mr. Knightley, Emma's sister's brother-in-law, has known Emma all her life. He is about sixteen years older than Emma and has been a kind of mentor to her throughout her life. Mr. Knightley berates Emma for what he considers to be her frivolous attention to matchmaking. He believes that her meddling in people's love lives may, in fact, cause irreparable harm. Harriet, he believes, would be much better served were Emma to encourage her to accept the marriage proposal of Robert Martin, a good and honest man who truly cares about her, than to raise her expectations above her station in life. Emma's relationship with Frank, he believes, brings out the worst in her, as is evidenced by the way in which they join forces to tease Miss Bates and Jane

Fairfax, two respectable women who suffer from poverty through no fault of their own. When Emma claims responsibility for the successful relationship between Mr. and Mrs. Weston, Mr. Knightley points out that she is taking credit for a relationship she merely observed happening, not one that she manipulated into being.

Mr. Knightley cares deeply about Emma. He has watched her grow from a young girl to a young woman. He understands her potential and wants to see her reach it. But more than that, Mr. Knightley has, without consciously acknowledging it to himself, fallen in love with Emma. His feelings of jealousy towards Frank Churchill (before he finds out that Frank's serious interests are with Jane Fairfax), together with his intense relief to find that Emma is not devastated by Frank's betrayal of her, causes him to recognize the truth of his feelings for the first time. And Emma, the young woman who has always believed she would never marry, recognizes her feelings of love for him when she begins to fear that he may be attaching himself elsewhere, first to Jane Fairfax, then Harriet Smith. The fear is short-lived, however, as Mr. Knightley expresses his love to Emma clearly and fully. Mr. Knightley proposes; Emma accepts; and the novel ends with three marriages being solemnized: Mr. Knightley to Emma Woodhouse, Jane Fairfax to Frank Churchill, and Robert Martin to Harriet Smith. The Weston wedding at the beginning of the novel was not the result of Emma's matchmaking, regardless of her attempts to take credit for it. Likewise, none of the three weddings at the end of the novel originate in the romantic manipulations of Emma Woodhouse. Emma's success rate as a matchmaker leaves much to be desired.

CHARACTER DEVELOPMENT

The novel *Emma*, unlike Jane Austen's earlier novels, does not focus the development of most of the characters in the novel around a single trait or pair of traits. Instead, it focuses primarily on the development of a single individual, Emma Woodhouse. At the beginning of the novel, Emma believes that, because of her social position and the deference most people show towards her as a result of it, she is capable of making good decisions on almost every subject. Taking on the task of matchmaking for members of her community is the most prominent example of her attempts to make decisions for those in her community, but it is not the only one. As the novel proceeds, the reader is led to have some serious doubts about Emma's decision-making abilities. Her motives are generally positive—she wants those in her community to be as comfortable, both physically and emotionally, as possible. But her judgment is often questionable. The novel is, in one sense, a novel of the education of a young woman. Through the process of interacting with others, and especially through her attempts to direct other people's lives, Emma gradually learns that her discernment about people is not as sound as she has thought. She learns, through a series of errors in judgment and personal disappointments, that meddling in the lives of others, especially when one does not have a clear understanding of their attitudes and experiences, causes problems more often than not.

Each of the characters in *Emma* is developed in relation to Emma's education. Mrs. Weston is the first character after Emma to be introduced, and her role as Emma's former governess introduces the themes of both education and judgment into the story. As Miss Taylor, Emma's governess had lived with the Woodhouse family for sixteen years. The relationship between Emma and Mrs. Weston, especially in the years since Emma's need for a governess has ended, has been "more the intimacy of sisters" than of mentor and student (1). Even "before Miss Taylor had ceased to hold the nominal office of governess," we are told, "the mildness of her temper had hardly allowed her to impose any restraint" (1). Since living together as friends, Emma has been "doing just what she liked; highly esteeming Miss Taylor's judgment, but directed chiefly by her own" (1). Thus, the woman whose job it is to educate Emma is too mild, even when Emma is very young, to restrain her from doing as she pleases, and Emma, while "highly esteeming Miss Taylor's judgment," acts only in accordance with her own, less-than-mature sense of discernment.

Mrs. Weston is a very good friend to Emma, but she, like almost everyone in Emma's life, permits Emma to have her own way much too often. She does not reprimand Emma when it is clear that she is behaving inappropriately. In fact, she is more likely to decide that Emma's judgment is correct than to trust her own.

Mr. Woodhouse, Emma's father, is not very helpful in developing Emma's ability to make mature and valid judgments either. His own judgment is flawed due to his intense hypochondria. Mr. Woodhouse considers every decision from only one angle—whether it could help or hurt someone's health. In her father Emma has the example of extremely short-sighted and narrow-minded judgment. She knows that he is unable to evaluate most situations properly. Therefore, she takes over much of the activity of running the household and making decisions for it. When a pig is slaughtered, Emma determines which portion to send to Mrs. Bates and her daughter as a much-needed gift. When social activities are suggested, Emma decides how best to accommodate her father's health and peace of mind. In a properly run family, the father would be training his children to make appropriate judgments; in the Woodhouse family, the child makes many of the decisions that traditionally fall to the father.

After Miss Taylor marries Mr. Weston and is no longer available as a daily companion, Emma finds another woman to share her days. Harriet Smith is seventeen years of age when Emma takes her up as a friend. The four years difference in their ages enables Emma to become Harriet's mentor more than would have been the case had they been the same age. Harriet was a very attractive girl whose "beauty happened to be of a sort which Emma particularly admired" (16). While her beauty first attracted Emma to her, it was her behavior that determined that Harriet would be Emma's daily companion. After spending an evening with her, Emma found that she

was not struck by any thing remarkably clever in Miss Smith's conversation, but she found her altogether very engaging—not inconveniently shy, not unwilling to talk—and yet so far from pushing, shewing so proper and becoming a deference, seeming so pleasantly grateful for being admitted to Hartfield, and so artlessly impressed by the appearance of every thing in so superior a style to what she had been used to, that she must have good sense and deserve encouragement. (16)

Harriet is, therefore, exactly the kind of friend she is looking for. Believing herself to be Harriet's superior in age, social status, and judgment, she believes that she is the person best suited to "encourage" Harriet. "It would," Emma tells herself, "be an interesting, and certainly a very kind undertaking; highly becoming her own situation in life, her leisure, and powers" (16). Emma's own lack of appropriate judgment, however, causes her to influence Harriet to give up her former friends and to learn to expect a higher place in society for herself than was her right by birth and upbringing. Emma thus raises unrealistic expectations in Harriet. She encourages her to believe that the town minister would be a good match, and when that proves to be untrue, still is not willing to allow Harriet to return to her former friends, the Martins. Instead she continues to encourage Harriet to expect attentions from other, more socially acceptable men. Harriet anticipates the attentions of both Frank Churchill and of Mr. George Knightley at different times in the course of the novel. These men are of a significantly higher social status than even the minister, Mr. Elton, yet Emma's insistence to Harriet that she is the equal of any man leads Harriet to expect such men to find her a potential mate. When those expectations are thwarted, Harriet feels deep disappointment. Emma finally acknowledges that she has been wrong in encouraging Harriet to expect attentions from men so far above her social station. Through her interaction with Harriet, she eventually learns how faulty her judgment has been. Her experiences with Harriet also teach her the dangers involved in trying to direct the emotions of others.

Emma learns another valuable lesson from her interaction with Miss Bates. Miss Bates is a poor woman, the daughter of the former rector of Highbury, who has never married. She lives with her mother in rooms they rent from one of the merchants in town. The Bates family had lived in the rectory and had a reasonably comfortable lifestyle while Mr. Bates was alive, but after his death, his widow and daughter were forced into significantly reduced circumstances. They remain eminently respectable women and are the object of charity by a number of the wealthier people in town (including the Knightleys and the Woodhouses).

Despite her reduced circumstances, Miss Bates is a woman who, as the narrator tells us, enjoys "a most uncommon degree of popularity for a woman neither young, handsome, rich, nor married" (14). She could boast neither "beauty or cleverness. Her youth had passed without distinction, and her middle of life was devoted to the care of a failing mother, and the endeavour to make a small income go as far as possible" (14). By all rights, Miss Bates might be expected to be a bitter woman. "And yet she was a happy woman, and a woman whom no one named without good-will" (14). Miss Bates is, in fact, appreciated by all in her community.

Miss Bates is extremely talkative. She is aware of that tendency but can rarely restrain herself. Generally people are very accepting and considerate of her long-winded stories. But Emma, on one occasion, allows her impatience with Miss Bates's tales to get the better of her. She, influenced by Frank Churchill, hurts Miss Bates's feelings quite badly by making what Emma thought at the time was a witty comment about the spinster's inability to stop talking. Miss Bates is horrified and blames herself for irritating Emma.

When Emma realizes how deeply Miss Bates's feelings have been hurt by her comment, she is sorry, but the damage has already been done. Mr. Knightley points out to her just how inappropriate her behavior has been.

How could you be so unfeeling to Miss Bates? How could you be so insolent in your wit to a woman of her character, age, and situation? . . . Were she a woman of fortune, I would leave every harmless absurdity to take its chance. I would not quarrel with you for any liberties of manner. Were she your equal in station—but, Emma, consider how far this is from being the case. She is poor; she has sunk from the comforts she was born to, and if she lives to old age, must probably sink more. Her situation should secure your compassion. . . . You, whom she had known from an infant, whom she had seen grow up from a period when her notice was an honour—to have you now, in thoughtless spirits, and the pride of the moment, laugh at her, humble her—and before her niece, too—and before others, many of whom (certainly *some*) would be entirely guided by *your* treatment of her." (303–304)

Mr. Knightley, unlike most of the people in Emma's life, is perfectly aware of her faults. He does not allow her to minimize the importance of her inconsiderate comment to Miss Bates. He makes certain that she understands just how inappropriate it is for her, *especially* for someone of her social standing and position, to make such a cruel comment to a woman who has suffered so much deprivation in her life already—through no fault of her own. Miss Bates herself would never dream of blaming Emma for making such a comment. She believes that she must be a torment for Emma to be around or Emma would not have said such a thing. But Mr. Knightley holds Emma responsible for her words and her actions. Through this incident Emma learns a very important lesson about the need to use good judgment at all times. She learns that a slip of the tongue in a moment of high spirits can cause tremendous damage. People of her standing in the community must be especially careful with every word and every action not to harm those who depend upon them for support and benevolent care.

Frank Churchill's contribution to Emma's education is as a negative example. Frank is essentially a spoiled little rich boy. He was adopted by his grandparents shortly after his mother's death, and has been raised in the comfort and luxury of their estate. That he will inherit the Churchill estate after his grandparents' death is certain. His future, therefore, is secure.

Emma's interest in Frank Churchill begins long before she meets him face to face. "[I]t so happened," the narrator tells us, "that in spite of Emma's resolution of never marrying, there was something in the name, in the idea of Mr. Frank Churchill, which always interested her" (95). In her thoughts on the matter, Emma decides that "if she *were* to marry, he [is] the very person to suit her in age, character, and condition" (95). With such high expectations, not only of the character of the young man she has yet to meet, but also of the inevitability of a significant relationship of some kind between them, Emma is primed for Frank's appearance in Highbury.

When Frank arrives, he appears to be everything that Emma expected. He is handsome and charming. His wealth is evident in all he does. And he pays Emma the attention that she feels she deserves. In fact, most in the neighborhood assume that an engagement between the two is forthcoming. But despite appearances, Frank is not free. He is secretly engaged to Jane Fairfax, and he uses his relationship with Emma to distract people from the relationship he cares most about. He uses Emma as a shield against the disfavor of his grandmother, while disregarding the pain such activity causes the woman he professes to love.

Frank's lack of consideration for others goes beyond Emma and Jane, however. He avoids visiting his father for many years, only appearing for the long-awaited visit when the presence of Jane Fairfax in Highbury gives him a selfish reason to come. He encourages Emma to ridicule those in Highbury who do not suit his own standards of behavior, people like the gentle Miss Bates. He arranges to have a piano delivered to Jane Fairfax, knowing that she will be hard-pressed to explain such an elaborate gift when their relationship cannot even be publicly acknowledged. He encourages Emma to believe that Jane may be in love with the man who married her best friend—when he knows full well where Jane's affections lie. All of these behaviors are unbecoming and improper. The fact that Emma allows herself to overlook those that she recognizes and to ignore, but be influenced by, the rest indicates just how much she has yet to learn about being an ethically proper young woman herself.

Mr. Knightley is the individual from whom Emma receives the most important lessons in her education in proper behavior. He is a strong man with a solid set of ethics as well as a substantial estate and income. He has been a close friend of the Woodhouse family all his life. His brother is married to Emma's sister, and he has acted much like an older brother to her throughout her life. Mr. Knightley is "one of the few people who could see faults in Emma Woodhouse, and the only one who ever told her of them" (6). While Emma does not enjoy hearing about her faults, she does admire and trust Mr. Knightley. As a result, she pays attention to what he has to say and tries, much of the time, to follow his advice. She counts on having him available to her and her father as counselor, friend, and business advisor. When Mrs. Weston suggests to Emma that Mr. Knightley may be falling in love with Jane Fairfax, Emma vehemently denies even the possibility: "Mr. Knightley and Jane Fairfax! . . . Dear Mrs. Weston, how could you think of such a thing? Mr. Knightley!—Mr. Knightley must not marry! . . . I cannot at all consent to Mr. Knightley's marrying; and I am sure it is not at all likely" (179–180). That Mr. Knightley would consider marrying, would consider an alliance with any family besides the Woodhouse family, is a thought beyond the realm of possibility for Emma. Yet, after Mrs. Weston suggests such a possibility, Emma cannot help but notice the attentions Mr. Knightley shows Jane Fairfax. She begins to believe that Mrs. Weston's views on the subject may not be as far from reality as she wants them to be. She begins to recognize, in her feelings of jealousy over Jane Fairfax, that her own feelings for Mr. Knightley are of a kind she has not been willing to acknowledge previously.

At the end of the novel, Mr. Knightley and Emma recognize that their attachment to each other is more than mere friendship, and Mr. Knightley asks Emma for her hand in marriage. She is both happy and relieved, but fears her father will not be willing to allow her to leave Hartfield. Mr. Knightley agrees that her father's wishes must be adhered to; in fact, he expresses pleasure that Emma shows such consideration for her father. They agree, therefore, to live together at Hartfield until such time as Mr. Woodhouse dies. At that time they will move to Donwell Abbey to live for the rest of their lives together. In this decision, Emma demonstrates proper judgment. She does not reject the offer of marriage from the man she loves, a man who seems to be the best suited man in all the world for her to marry. But she also does not desert her father, a man who depends on her presence for his support and comfort each day of his life.

In the course of the novel Emma grows from a young woman who believes that she knows better than anyone else in her neighborhood what is best for individual community members into a more mature woman who has suffered disappointments and has come to understand that individuals need to handle their own relationships, make their own choices, and enjoy their triumphs or suffer negative consequences as the result of their own actions. She learns that she must take care of her own life and that, in paying attention to her own behavior, she can operate as a guide to ethical behavior by modeling it. Emma learns to be considerate of others without feeling the need to take over their lives and make their decisions for them.

THEMATIC CONCERNS

Two themes predominate in *Emma*: the importance of right action (ethical behavior) and the dangers of trying to raise oneself out of one's social status. These themes are often interrelated in the novel as much of the action that is not ethical is related to the attempts of people to raise themselves or others into inappropriate social positions.

Right action is represented first and foremost by Mr. Knightley. He recognizes his own place at the top of the social order in Highbury and accepts that such a position requires him to behave according to an impeccable standard of ethics. As he points out to Emma following her insulting comments to Miss Bates, she, as a leading member of society in Highbury, has a responsibility to behave with impeccability in order to guide the behavior of others as well as simply because it is right to do so. Mr. Knightley takes his role as a leading member of Highbury society seriously. He assists those of his community who deserve it and behaves towards everyone with as good a heart as possible. Mr. Knightley recognizes and appreciates right action in people of all walks of life, not merely those at the top of the social ladder. He encourages a relationship between Harriet Smith and Robert Martin not only because Robert is better suited to Harriet's social status than Mr. Elton, Frank Churchill, or himself; but because Robert is a very good man who takes his family and occupational responsibilities seriously.

Mr. Knightley is also the leading proponent in the novel of the need for people to remain in the social position that has been determined by their birth. By more democratic twenty-first-century standards, such a position seems in direct opposition to the rule of right action, but at the time Austen was writing, it was a much more common perspective. Although not the only questionable aspect of Emma's matchmaking, her desire to help Harriet raise herself out of the situation into which she has been born is one of the most problematical. Harriet's parentage is unknown. She is almost certainly illegitimate. She has been educated in a small, unprestigious girls' boarding school. She is not particularly clever or endowed with any attributes beyond beauty and a pleasant personality. Robert Martin, a local farmer with a generous heart and a willingness to work hard to support his widowed mother, sisters, and a wife, is a perfect mate for her according to the social standards of the day. That Harriet is already good friends with his sisters and that she and Robert truly care for each other are additional factors in favor of their union. Such a marriage, the novel implies, has an excellent chance of promoting the happiness of those involved.

Mr. Knightley and Emma Woodhouse are also well-suited as marriage partners. The sixteen-year difference in their ages could present some difficulties, but such age differences, especially in marriages at their level of society, were quite common and seemed to work well in the eighteenth century. Emma and Mr. Knightley are members of the two most prominent families in their neighborhood. Their estates are adjoining and, if combined (as is likely after Mr. Woodhouse's death) will provide extremely well for any children they may have. Even separately, Mr. Knightley and Miss Woodhouse are looked up to as the leading forces in Highbury society; their marriage simply solidifies those positions. Emma may still have some growing up to do after marriage, but the responsibility she has held for several years as mistress of her father's house, together with the lessons she has learned in right action in the course of the novel, indicates that she and Mr. Knightley will, indeed, create a very successful partnership.

The third marriage that occurs at the end of the book does not bode as well. Frank Churchill and Jane Fairfax are both children of military officers, a fact that should place them on an equal footing, but the differences in the lives they have lived are likely to cause difficulty in their marriage. Frank, although born into a military family, was taken soon after his birth into a very wealthy family to be raised as their adopted son. He is raised with all the privileges of high social position and with the expectation that he will be the sole inheritor of the vast Churchill estate. Frank's upbringing, despite his social position at birth, is that of the elder son of an extremely wealthy family. Jane Fairfax, on the other hand, loses her parents at a very young age and is left to depend upon her grandmother, the poor widow of a minister. She is fortunate to be taken by her father's friend, Mr. Campbell, and raised with his daughter, by which means she becomes genteelly educated. Nonetheless Jane is aware that her future is not secure, that she has no family of fortune to fall back on. The resulting disparity between Jane Fairfax and Frank Churchill creates a situation in which Frank, as the spoiled adopted heir to a grand estate, cannot understand the pain he causes his fiancée by what he considers to be good-natured teasing, and

Jane, as a woman who has always been aware that her position is precarious, assumes prematurely that Frank does not intend to follow through with the marriage he has promised her. The disparity between their positions is not sufficient to consider the match inappropriate, but it does indicate that they may suffer greater disagreements and misunderstandings than marital partners who have been raised in more similar surroundings.

A FEMINIST READING OF THE CHARACTER OF EMMA WOODHOUSE

Feminist interpretative approaches can be used to illuminate ideas about women and their position in society within novels that are not always clear from a superficial reading. Those ideas are sometimes expressed through background stories or plot development. Often, however, they are most fully developed through characters' motivations and behavior. Such is the case with Jane Austen's novel *Emma*, in which much of the critique of eighteenth-century marriage laws and customs is centered in the character of Emma Woodhouse.

In *Emma*, Austen creates a heroine who does not need to be married in order to have a secure life. Emma Woodhouse is her father's heir. She is, even as an unmarried twenty-one-year-old woman, the preeminent woman in Highbury society. As a result, she does not aspire to marriage as a way to provide herself with greater security or greater social position.

On the surface, *Emma* appears to be a very conservative novel. It does not promote the idea of raising oneself above one's station in society or seem to advocate changing the status quo in any way. In the character of Emma Woodhouse, however, Austen relates a more subversive message. The women's rights novels of the late eighteenth century promoted the idea that marriage placed women in a position of bondage and reduced their legal identity to that of being the property of their husbands. Emma's views towards a marriage for herself coincides, to a great extent, with that view. By examining Emma's words and actions through the lens of feminist criticism, we can more clearly detect Austen's critique of the marriage laws of her time.

Emma is the one and only young unmarried woman in all of Austen's fiction who does not aspire to marriage. She, like Charlotte Lucas in *Pride and Prejudice*, seems to believe that happiness in marriage is a matter of chance, but unlike Charlotte, she does not need a marriage in order to be secure financially. She does not aspire to greater wealth or social position within her community, since she is already a member of the most prominent family in the neighborhood. She does not wish for greater influence regarding the business of an estate since she already has great influence in the management of her father's estate. Her older sister has provided a male heir; therefore, she has no need to marry and produce children in order to satisfy some sense of familial continuity. Emma recognizes that she has no practical reason to marry, that, in fact, her independence would be seriously impinged upon if she were to marry.

The novel opens with a description of Emma's domestic situation: "Emma Woodhouse, handsome, clever, and rich, with a comfortable home and happy disposition, seemed to unite some of the best blessings of existence; and had lived nearly twenty-one years in the world with very little to distress or vex her" (1). She is "the youngest of the two daughters of a most affectionate, indulgent father" and has been mistress of his home since she was twelve years old (1). Because of this combination of circumstances, she experiences no restrictions in her life as an unmarried daughter that would be alleviated if she were married. Emma explains her position to Harriet Smith who wonders why Emma is not yet engaged to be married:

I am not only, not going to be married, at present, but have very little intention of ever marrying at all. . . . I must see somebody very superior to any one I have seen yet, to be tempted . . . and I do *not* wish to see any such person. I would rather not be tempted. I cannot really change for the better. If I were to marry, I must expect to repent it. (67)

The change Emma refers to is situational, not personal. As the wealthy daughter of an indulgent, sickly father who allows her to manage his household and, to a great extent, even his estate, Emma sees little personal benefit in marriage. In fact, she does not even want to be tempted to marry. She knows that she is more independent as her father's daughter than she would be as almost anyone's wife. When Harriet expresses surprise at Emma's position, Emma elaborates:

I have none of the usual inducements of women to marry. Were I to fall in love, indeed, it would be a different thing! but I never have been in love; it is not my way, or my nature, and I do not think I ever shall. And without love, I am sure I should be a fool to change such a situation as mine. Fortune I do not want; employment I do not want; consequence I do not want: I believe few married women are half as much mistress of their husband's house, as I am of Hartfield; and never, never could I expect to be so truly beloved and important; so always first and always right in any man's eyes as I am in my father's. (67–68)

Emma understands her situation clearly at this point. She wrongly believes that falling in love is not her "nature," but she correctly believes that she would sacrifice her independence by becoming a wife in a traditional marriage.

Harriet continues to protest against Emma's attitude, however, asserting that to be "an old maid" is "so dreadful" a fate that Emma cannot seriously consider it (68). But Emma, once again, makes a clear distinction between her situation and that of other women: "I shall not be a poor old maid; and it is poverty only which makes celibacy contemptible to a generous public . . . a single woman, of good fortune, is always respectable, and may be as sensible and pleasant as anybody else" (68). Emma's fortune would prevent her from becoming a burden on the community as a spinster; it would enable her to lead an active life of useful employment, to enjoy family and community connections without having to become dependent on those connections for her livelihood. Emma recognizes that her financial and familial position is especially fortunate. She knows that most women do not have her options.

In areas other than marriage, Emma's attitudes and actions also differ significantly from those of members of other property-owning families in Austen's fiction. Because she has no brother to inherit her father's estate and her father's invalid condition allows him to excuse himself from managing the estate personally, Emma, as mistress of the estate, often acts in his stead. She is the true decision maker in the family. Her father plays the more passive, traditionally feminine role.

Because Mr. Woodhouse has abdicated his position of responsibility in the community and has allowed Emma to act in his place, Emma is allowed many of the prerogatives of maleness in her community. For example, she is considerably more interested in and cognizant of the politics of estate business than her father, as is demonstrated by the conversation at Hartfield when John and Isabella Knightley visit. While Mr. Woodhouse and Isabella discuss physicians, children, and health, all traditionally female subjects, Emma involves herself with the Knightley brothers in a traditionally male discussion of local politics and estate management. "I did not thoroughly understand what you were telling your brother," cried Emma, "about your friend Mr. Graham's intending to have a bailiff from Scotland, to look after his new estate. But will it answer? Will not the old prejudice be too strong?" (83). Emma's questions indicate not only her interest in the subject, but also her understanding of the nationalist prejudices that affect the administration of estates. And, so that we do not think this comment an isolated insight, the narrator informs us that Emma "talked in this way . . . long and successfully" (83). The implications are twofold: first, that Emma can participate intelligently and fully in a discussion of estate business and politics; and second, that the traditionally female topics of health, children, and doctors do not interest her. Emma's intellectual interests are those that are considered to be more traditionally masculine than feminine.

Emma does not, however, enjoy all of the privileges that men of property in her time relish. Because she is female, society does not allow her the same freedom of movement and independence that sons of landed property have. Although she suffers few restrictions because of her gender within her father's home and the community of Highbury, Emma is fully aware, as every woman of her society must be, that her freedom of movement and activity in the world beyond Highbury is severely restricted.

Emma's initial determination not to marry, even after realizing that she is in love with Mr. Knightley, demonstrates her recognition that a traditional marriage would prevent her from filling the role she has been playing in her family, the role traditionally filled by the eldest son and heir. Although she realizes how dear Mr. Knightley is to her, she would still prefer not to marry him. Emma enjoys her relationship with Mr. Knightley as it stands. She does not want to exchange her position as unmarried mistress of the Hartfield estate for that of the married mistress of Donwell Abbey (337). She rationalizes her preference by determining that marriage would "be incompatible with what she owed her father, and with what she felt for him" (338). Marriage, therefore, "would not do for her. . . . Nothing should separate her from her father" (338). To Emma's credit, she does understand her father well. If she were to marry, particularly if she were to marry and move away from Hartfield, his life and peace of mind would be disrupted. On the other hand, Emma also must recognize that marrying Mr. Knightley and moving to his home would significantly alter her own life as well. She would no longer be able to act as head of the estate in her father's place; instead she would fill the much more conventional position of wife to an active landowner. Her activities would probably become more domestic, forcing her to occupy the traditionally feminine realm much more exclusively than she has as an unmarried woman. She would be forced to adapt to her husband's home, habits, and schedule rather than being able to lead her own relatively independent life in a home she manages. Consideration of these potential limitations upon her life as a married woman, as well as her understanding that if she marries she loses all legal control of her own property, undoubtedly contributes to her determination not to marry.

Emma does, however, agree to marry Mr. Knightley. Her love for him and excitement over discovering that her love is reciprocated make it impossible for her to refuse him. The fact that she accepts Mr. Knightley's proposal does not mean, however, that she has decided to live the life of the traditional wife of a man of property: "She hardly knew yet what Mr. Knightley would ask, but a very short parley with her own heart produced the most solemn resolution of never quitting her father. . . . While he lived it must be only an engagement" (353). The thought of leaving her father and, by implication, Hartfield itself, saddens Emma. An engagement binds Mr. Knightley to her. It does not, however, restrict her legally or personally in the ways that marriage would. With an engagement, Emma could remain single with all the advantages of that state, while being assured of the continuing love and support of the man she loves.

When Emma tells Mr. Knightley that she cannot marry while her father lives, he provides an alternative. Instead of taking Emma from her father's home, her husband will agree to move in with them. He will live there until such time as Mr. Woodhouse dies, at which point he and his wife will move to his family home, Donwell Abbey, for the remainder of their lives. Mr. Knightley's suggestion that he move into Hartfield instead of forcing Emma to leave her father's home may appear to be merely the most rational alternative, but it is, in fact, quite an unusual decision for the time. Emma recognizes that "in quitting Donwell, he must be sacrificing a great deal of independence of hours and habits; that in living constantly with her father, and in no house of his own, there would be much, very much to be borne with" (366). For Mr. Knightley, a man who is accustomed to being the head of his own household, the master of his own estate, to move into the home which his wife has already been mistress of for many years, a home of which her father remains the master, requires great self-sacrifice. Mr. Knightley is, in every sense but legal, agreeing to put himself into the traditional position of a wife while allowing his wife to continue the life to which she has been accustomed.

The time period in which Jane Austen wrote was a time in which successful novels ended in the marriage of the heroine to the hero. Novels that overtly challenged the importance of marriage in the lives of women were reminders of the women's rights novels of two decades past, novels that were considered downright obscene to most publishers and readers of the early nineteenth century. Austen could not, therefore, successfully publish a novel which overtly rejected marriage—even if she had wanted to do so. But the criticisms Emma makes of marriage as an institution, together with the fact that the marriage she finally agrees to is not a traditional marriage, provides a less comfortable view of marriage than Austen is often assumed to present. *Emma* is not stridently and rigidly against the entire institution of marriage, as are novels by Mary Wollstonecraft and Mary Hays, but it does address many of the same issues they do in a more palatable and gentler fashion.

7

Northanger Abbey
(1818)

Northanger Abbey has the distinction of being Jane Austen's first sold but last published book. According to Cassandra Austen, Jane's sister, it was written in 1798 and 1799 and sold to the publisher Crosby and Co. in 1803. At that time its title was *Susan*. As Austen continued writing her other novels, she awaited the publication of her first novel, but even though advertisements for the novel appeared in popular periodicals, publication never happened. Austen wrote the publisher in 1809, demanding immediate publication or the right to publish elsewhere. Crosby and Co. threatened her with a lawsuit if she tried to place the manuscript with a different publisher, but continued to postpone publishing the book. In 1816, after four of her novels had already been published, Austen arranged for her brother Henry to buy back the manuscript from Crosby and Co. They, unaware that the anonymous manuscript they held was written by the author of the best-selling *Pride and Prejudice* and *Sense and Sensibility*, sold it back to him for what they had paid for it.

During the last years of her life, Austen revised *Susan* into *Northanger Abbey*. She changed the heroine's name and added some references that would not have been available to her before 1803, but there is no evidence that her revision of the novel was extensive. Unlike *Sense and Sensibility* and *Pride and Prejudice*, both of which underwent changes in form as well as content when revised from their original state, *Northanger Abbey* remains very close to the original in both form and content. In fact, her changes were so minimal that she felt it necessary to explain the novel's publication history in an advertisement she prepared for release about the novel:

This little work was finished in the year 1803, and intended for immediate publication. It was disposed of to a bookseller, it was even advertised, and why the business proceeded no farther, the author has never been able to learn. . . . The public are entreated to bear in mind that thirteen years have passed since it was finished, many more since it was begun, and that during that period, places, manners, books, and opinions have undergone considerable changes. (xxxiii *Northanger Abbey*, Oxford University Edition)

Austen lived long enough to complete her revisions of *Northanger Abbey* and even to write the advertisement for the novel, but she did not live to see it published. After her death in 1817, Cassandra and Henry were left with two completed manuscripts, *Northanger Abbey* and *Persuasion*. They arranged for her publisher to bring out these final two novels posthumously.

Northanger Abbey is very different in tone and structure from Austen's other novels. Whereas her other novels explore the minds and hearts of their major characters in considerable depth, *Northanger Abbey* focuses on a combination of plot and an examination of literary forms. Catherine Morland, the heroine of the novel, is a unifying force, but she never comes alive to the reader in the same way that Elizabeth Bennet, Fanny Price, or Emma Woodhouse do. She is more a type of young woman than a fully developed character in her own right.

That the characters are not as fully developed as in Austen's other novels has caused some critics to consider *Northanger Abbey* a less well-crafted and less important novel than the others. But this novel is not a novel of character. Instead it provides a commentary on the literature of England at the end of the eighteenth century. In a very real sense, *Northanger Abbey* represents Austen's placement of herself and her novels within the literary context of her time.

PLOT SUMMARY

Northanger Abbey opens by introducing the reader to the heroine of the novel, Catherine Morland. Catherine, we are told, is the heroine even though "[n]o one who [had] ever seen [her] in her infancy, would have supposed her born to be a heroine" (1). The narrator continues, pointing out that Catherine had a good home, a good father, nine brothers and sisters, and a happy childhood. She was not a particularly attractive girl, nor did she have an excessive amount of charm, talent, or intelligence. In other words, Catherine Morland is an ordinary English girl, not an author's typical choice for the heroine of a novel.

Once the narrator establishes the unlikelihood of a girl like Catherine being chosen for a heroine, the action begins. Mr. Allen, a local man of property, is directed by his physician to go to Bath for his health. His wife, who enjoys Catherine's company and does not want to go to Bath alone with her husband, invites her along. Catherine's parents agree, and the fifteen-year-old Catherine takes off for a youthful adventure in the resort town of Bath.

The Allens introduce Catherine into society in Bath. They attend balls and parties in various of the public rooms, where Catherine initially feels very uncomfortable. She knows no one in the town, nor do the Allens. Catherine, therefore, spends much of her time at her first dance in Bath feeling disoriented and out of place. Within a few days, however, her situation improves. The master of ceremonies at the Lower Rooms, one of the public rooms at Bath, introduces her to a young gentleman by the name of Henry Tilney. They dance together, go to tea, and spend considerable time chatting. Tilney is about twenty-five years old, considerably older and more knowledgeable about the world than young Catherine. He enjoys acting as though he is quite jaded, asking all the questions one is expected to ask of a new acquaintance one meets at a dance with a satiric and even, at times, cynical tone of voice. Catherine does not understand why he speaks in the manner he does or what he can find so humorous about her straightforward replies to his questions. Her youth and innocence are qualities he finds appealing in a town where so many of the young women he meets are completely artificial in their talk and behavior.

Catherine is excited after her evening with Henry Tilney. She looks forward to seeing him again the next day, but although she looks for him throughout the streets of Bath and in the public rooms, she does not find him.

Meanwhile, Mrs. Allen finally meets an acquaintance, a woman by the name of Mrs. Thorpe. Mrs. Thorpe is a widow with several children, two of whom, Isabella and John, are of an age to socialize with Catherine. After talking with John for a while, Catherine discovers that he is a schoolmate of her older brother. She feels an immediate rapport with him and his sister because of that association.

The Allens and the Thorpes spend part of almost every day together, but although Catherine is kept very busy with her new friends, she continues to look for Henry Tilney. She cannot forget the first young man to dance with her at Bath. She takes walks, exchanges gossip, and even reads novels with Isabella. She rides out in a carriage with the young Thorpes as well as going to dances and teas with them in the public rooms. But always she is alert for any sign of Mr. Tilney.

Catherine's brother James comes to Bath to visit with John Thorpe, and together the four young people explore Bath and its environs. In the course of their adventures, it becomes clear that Isabella and James are closer than they had at first revealed. James encourages Catherine's friendship with Isabella, praising the young Miss Thorpe at every opportunity. Catherine, young and naïve, remains unaware of the degree of her brother's affection for her new friend for quite some time.

The Thorpe and Allen parties often go to the Lower Rooms in the evening for dancing and socializing. On those occasions James and Isabella are partnered with each other as are John and Catherine. On one such occasion, however, John goes to the card room immediately after their arrival, leaving Catherine waiting for him in the ballroom. Isabella at first refuses to desert her friend, but James finally convinces her to leave Catherine and dance with him. Catherine is left sitting on the sidelines, abandoned both by the man who had promised to partner her and by her friend who might otherwise have kept her company. She again feels the discomfort she had felt on her first visit to the hall.

Suddenly she sees Mr. Tilney standing nearby, talking with a young woman. Mr. Tilney approaches Catherine and introduces her to his sister. He explains that he has been away from Bath, having left the morning after they danced together. He asks Catherine to dance, but she is obliged to refuse him, having already promised to dance with John Thorpe. When John returns from the card room a few minutes later, he finds Catherine rather irritated with his behavior and not pleased by any part of his explanation—which is essentially that he found himself enjoying conversation with some of his gentlemen friends too fully to want to leave them even to dance with her.

By the end of the evening, Catherine manages to become much better acquainted with Miss Tilney. She finds her to be very attractive, quite elegant, and much more genuinely gracious than Isabella. She appreciates her new acquaintance for those qualities, along with the added bonus of her being Henry Tilney's sister.

Over the weeks to come, the Thorpes and her brother James continue to occupy as much of Catherine's time as they possibly can, but Catherine no longer enjoys the time she spends with them as much as she had before. Her strongest desire is to become better acquainted with Miss Tilney and her brother. She is kept from doing so, however, as John Thorpe whisks her away for various adventures in the company of his sister and her brother. Catherine, so young and good-hearted, tries to avoid such adventures, but finds that resisting the pressure of the three young people without the assistance of an adult (the Allens are both too preoccupied with their own activities to attend to Catherine's needs) is too difficult.

Finally, Catherine does manage to avoid the Thorpes long enough to become better acquainted with Miss Tilney and her brother. She even manages to dance with Mr. Tilney again, a treat she has been looking forward to since the first night they met. Mr. Tilney continues to speak in a manner that reveals a rather cynical wit, but Catherine recognizes the charm of a genuinely good man behind the sophisticated banter. Whereas John Thorpe often says the right thing but behaves inconsiderately towards her, Henry Tilney speaks at time almost in riddles, but behaves with the utmost gallantry and gentlemanliness towards her. Catherine intuitively knows the difference.

The Thorpes continue to cause Catherine difficulties. They sometimes prevent her from meeting with Miss Tilney when she has made plans to do so, and at one point John even lies to Miss Tilney when he is determined to spend the day with Catherine against her wishes. When Catherine finds out about the deception, she is horrified. She fears that the Tilneys will never forgive her for what appears to be double-dealing on her own part. Catherine apologizes profusely to Henry when next she sees him. Her regret is so clear that he cannot help but to forgive her and to tell her that he will explain the situation to his sister for her. Thus, what began as an incident which Catherine feared would part her from the Tilneys forever ends up becoming something that ultimately brings them even closer.

Over the next few days, Catherine is invited to the Tilney's house where she meets Eleanor and Henry's father, General Tilney. The General is extremely gracious towards her and encourages the development of a further friendship between her and his children. They continue to develop that friendship by going on long walks together, discussing subjects as diverse as politics, literature, and history, and spending time together in the most fashionable haunts of Bath.

The Thorpes continue pressing Catherine to spend time with them, but she avoids them as much as she can without offending them horribly. She no longer rides out in the carriage with John Thorpe, but she and Isabella continue to get together at times to talk with each other. During one of these friendly conversations, Isabella reveals to Catherine that she and James, Catherine's brother, are engaged to be married. She asks Catherine how she thinks her parents will respond to the news. Catherine, who has never contemplated such a turn of events, is quite excited to think that her friend will soon be a member of her family. She cannot imagine that her parents will object to the plan.

James Morland goes home to ask his parents' consent for his engagement to Isabella. Although Catherine assures Isabella that he will get it, Isabella is concerned that the smallness of her fortune may cause them to refuse. What Catherine in her naïveté does not understand is that Isabella's fears are based on her misconception that James will inherit a significant fortune. Had Catherine realized the implications of Isabella's comments, she probably would have suspected that her desire to marry James was based on economic considerations at least as much as on affection and a desire to spend a lifetime with him.

Within a couple of days, James sends a letter to Isabella confirming his parents' consent to the engagement. Isabella considers the matter closed, certain that along with their consent will come the wealth that she has anticipated since first setting her sights on her brother's schoolmate. So ends the first volume of *Northanger Abbey*.

The second volume of the novel opens with Catherine visiting the Tilney family at their house in Bath. Catherine has anticipated the visit as an opportunity to get much better acquainted with both Eleanor and Henry Tilney. She is, however, disappointed. Although she cannot determine the cause, she finds both the brother and sister less forthcoming and less comfortable conversing with her in their own home than in public. And although she admits to herself that General Tilney "was perfectly agreeable and good-natured, and altogether a charming man," she feels that "it had been a release to get away from him" (100). Despite such a disconcerting visit, Catherine continues to look forward to getting to know the Tilneys better.

Henry and Eleanor Tilney have an older brother who is a professional military man. Captain Tilney arrives in Bath at this point in the story to spend some time with his family. When they arrive at the Lower Rooms on the evening of his arrival, Captain Tilney arranges to have his brother Henry introduce him to Isabella so that he might ask her to dance. Since Isabella previously declared to Catherine her determination not to dance with anyone since she is now an engaged woman and James has not yet returned from his visit to his parents, Catherine is stunned when Isabella accepts Captain Tilney's offer. She continues, despite her experience of the Thorpes, to expect both Isabella and John to behave in accordance with their words. Each time they fail to do so, Catherine is surprised by their inconstancy.

A second letter arrives from James, detailing the assistance his parents are able to give him so that he may marry Isabella. The results are far from satisfactory to the Thorpes. They, believing still that the Morlands are wealthy, are disappointed at both the amount of income James will receive as well as the fact that he will have to wait two and a half to three years, until he is ordained, to receive it. Catherine is hurt by the insinuations of the Thorpes that her father is doing less for the young couple than he could, but she still does not realize that Isabella and her family have a dramatically inflated idea of what her father is worth.

The six weeks that the Allens had intended to spend in Bath draw to a close, and discussion of returning home begins. Catherine hates the idea of having to end her acquaintance with the Tilneys so soon. It turns out, however, that the Tilneys are also at the end of their time in Bath and are planning to return soon to their home, Northanger Abbey. Eleanor Tilney, with her father's express approval, invites Catherine to go home with them for a visit before returning to her parents' home. The General has already spoken to Mr. and Mrs. Allen about the possibility, and they seem to think there will be no difficulty getting Mr. and Mrs. Morland's permission for the visit. Catherine assures the Tilneys that she will write her parents immediately for permission. Permission arrives, and Catherine prepares to travel with the Tilneys to Northanger Abbey.

Before leaving for Northanger Abbey, Catherine meets with Isabella, who has been instructed by her brother to sound Catherine out about her interest in a serious relationship with him. She is astonished to find that he could possibly have any such thoughts and assures Isabella that, not only has she never thought of John romantically, but that she never will do so. Isabella seems to believe that Catherine has led her brother on, but claims not to blame her for changing her mind now. "Take my word for it," Isabella tells Catherine, "if you are in too great a hurry [to get engaged], you will certainly live to regret it" (115). Isabella's own regret is clear to the reader who sees her with Captain Tilney and realizes that she wishes to be free to attach herself to him. Catherine notices Tilney's attentiveness to Isabella and fears he may be falling in love with her, but she thinks too well of people, and most especially of her friends, to think that Isabella could be encouraging his attentions consciously.

Catherine leaves Bath with some reservations about her friend's attachment to her brother, but her thoughts of Isabella, James, and Captain Tilney fall away as she travels with the Tilneys towards the Abbey. Catherine talks with Henry about his family home, revealing her assumptions that, because it is an abbey, it is old, decaying, and quite picturesque. Henry plays with her assumptions, suggesting the possibility of haunted corridors, secret sliding panels, and mysterious appearances and disappearances. He suggests numerous scenarios from gothic novels, all of which, he implies, could happen to her in the Abbey. She is greatly surprised, therefore, when she arrives at the Abbey only to find that it is a very modern building with no sign of gothic mystery about it at all.

Catherine's visit at Northanger Abbey puts her in daily contact with General Tilney. As was true of her earlier experience of him, the General remains quite cordial. He shows concern that she finds her room satisfactory and that she finds the Abbey itself to be to her liking. But she also is exposed to the General's rigid rule of his home. Meals are to be served at a designated time, and no one is permitted to arrive late to them. Certain parts of the house are off-limits to all residents. Catherine realizes that the General's very presence puts a pall over the spirits of his children, and although she cannot determine exactly what it is about him that does so, she recognizes its effect even on herself.

Catherine continues to be influenced by her gothic reading as she views the Abbey. She imagines that the large cabinet in her bedroom could contain something of interest. Therefore, during a storm (the perfect accompaniment to a gothic adventure), she searches each of its compartments and finally finds a rolled-up bunch of papers, a manuscript that she imagines contains clues to a mystery or letters passed between lovers forbidden to see each other. Just as she prepares to read the manuscript, her candle goes out, leaving her in the dark, in a storm, with an imagination full of gothic horrors.

In the morning when Catherine is finally able to read the pages from the cabinet, she is terribly disappointed to find that they contain only an inventory of linen. The mysterious manuscript which had filled her imagination throughout the night is, in fact, as mundane as the modern rooms in the Abbey. She thinks back to the way Henry Tilney had encouraged her to indulge her imagination on the way to the Abbey and decides to keep the knowledge of her foolishness from him. She refuses to give him a good laugh at her expense.

The morning after the storm, Henry leaves Northanger to go to Woodston where he serves as rector. He spends at least a couple of days each week in residence at Woodston so that he can fulfill his obligations to his parish. The General explains to Catherine how important he thinks it is for a man to have a profession, even if he does not need one in order to support himself. "The money," General Tilney insists, "is nothing, it is not an object, but employment is the thing" (141). General Tilney has seen too many young men without professions who ride around the countryside or idle away in the city, getting themselves into trouble with gambling, drink, and/or women. A man with a profession, on the other hand, while he may find some time and energy to get himself in trouble, has responsibilities to fulfill. He is less likely, therefore, to attract trouble than his idle counterpart. General Tilney has insisted that his sons have professions. His eldest son, Frederick, has followed his father's lead and entered the military. Henry is a clergyman.

Although each attempt on Catherine's part to find a gothic secret in the Abbey has thus far failed, she has not yet learned her lesson. Her imagination continues to work overtime. Upon learning that the late Mrs. Tilney died in the Abbey and surmising that the relationship between the General and his late wife was not a particularly loving one, Catherine begins to imagine another gothic plot, the murder of Mrs. Tilney by the General. When she discovers that Mrs. Tilney's illness was "sudden and short" and that Eleanor was away from home when her mother died, "Catherine's blood ran cold with the horrid suggestions which naturally sprang from these words" (150). Nature, of course, has nothing to do with it. Catherine's suspicions have been formed by her reading of gothic literature, not by any natural occurrences in her experience.

Catherine's latest suspicions are also proven false. Henry Tilney was present at his mother's death, and he assures Catherine that she died of a natural illness. Catherine has difficulty believing him at first but finally is forced to accept that, while General Tilney is indeed guilty of not being a very loving and affectionate husband, he did not murder his wife.

Henry Tilney forces Catherine to see just how fully she has been allowing her imagination to run away with her. That she could be so certain in her mind that the man who is her host could be the murderer of his wife is, she realizes, quite horrible. General Tilney, for all his rigidity and lack of social grace and charm, has treated Catherine with exceptional courtesy and generosity ever since she met him. Henry asks that she remember his treatment of her and then judge herself for harboring such suspicions of a man who has treated her so well. The narrator informs us that Catherine's "visions of romance were over," that she "was completely awakened" from her gothic imaginings after Henry's response to her suspicions (160).

A letter arrives at Northanger Abbey for Catherine. It is from her brother James who informs her that Isabella has broken off their engagement. She plans now, it seems, to marry Captain Tilney. Catherine is surprised that Isabella could betray her brother. She shares the information with Eleanor and Henry, feeling that they should know the history of their sister-in-law to be. They both assure her that it is extremely unlikely that Frederick has any intention of marrying the fortuneless Isabella. He has, it seems, a history of such dalliances. Both Eleanor and Henry assure Catherine that she is better off without Isabella in her family, that Isabella appears to be a fortune hunter and that the likelihood is that Isabella will marry the richest man she can land. They also agree that a woman as poor as Isabella would never be accepted by the General as a prospective daughter-in-law.

When alone, Catherine contemplates all that Eleanor and Henry have said. She realizes that she is "as insignificant, and perhaps as portionless as Isabella," and if, she thinks, Frederick does not have the "grandeur and wealth" on his own merits to marry a woman of little fortune, how much less would his younger brother be able to afford such a marriage (168). She thinks about the encouragement she has felt from General Tilney that has caused her to imagine that she and Henry might someday marry and finds it hard to believe that he could be so prejudiced against a woman without fortune as his children assume he would be.

Time passes. A trip is planned and executed to go to Woodston to see Henry's rectory, which Catherine finds to be quite charming. The General continues to address Catherine with the utmost affection, looking to her for approval of his plans, his home, and his children. When he is called to London for a week or so, he leaves, "earnestly regretting that any necessity should rob him even for an hour of Miss Morland's company" (178).

A few days later, the General unexpectedly returns to the Abbey. Eleanor comes to Catherine's room with the news that Catherine must leave Northanger first thing the next morning. Her excuse is that the General has just remembered a prior engagement for the family and that they must prepare to leave home immediately. Eleanor is quite shaken and apologetic as she gives Catherine the news. It is clear from her demeanor that the reason Catherine must leave has nothing to do with a prior engagement. Something the General learned while in London is the cause of his despicable treatment of his guest.

Catherine is sent home the next morning without even a servant for protection. Eleanor, fortunately, realizes that Catherine may not have money for such a trip, having been already so long away from home. Catherine, who had not even considered such a difficulty, accepts the money Eleanor so graciously offers, and, without further interaction with the General or Henry Tilney, who is in Woodston and ignorant of her dismissal from his father's house, begins her journey home.

Catherine arrives home safely, having experienced no difficulties on the journey. Her family is thrilled to have her home, though quite surprised to have her arrive in a coach, alone, so unexpectedly. She tells the story Eleanor had told her, of an engagement being remembered which forced her to be sent home, and her family, while judging General Tilney's behavior to be inappropriate in sending her home alone without even notifying her family, accepts the story as truth.

After a few days, during which Catherine experiences unusually low spirits, a visitor arrives. It is Henry Tilney. He apologizes for his sudden appearance, assuring them that he will understand if the family is unwilling to have him visit, considering the way his father treated Catherine. But his concern that Catherine has arrived home safely has overwhelmed every other sensation. After a few minutes of uncomfortable conversation with Mrs. Morland, Henry and Catherine go outdoors, where they can talk with some degree of privacy.

Henry proposes marriage to Catherine. He states clearly that he does not have his father's approval, that in fact his father has "ordered him to think of her no more" (199). He also reveals the reason that the General sent Catherine from his home in so unseemly a manner. While absent from home, the General had discovered that he had been misled about her wealth. While still in Bath, John Thorpe had bragged to the General about the fortune that Catherine Morland would bring to the husband she married. At the time Thorpe planned on being that husband. His information had, of course, been false. He had believed the Morlands to be wealthier than they are, and in his vanity, he enjoyed representing the family he planned to marry into as even more prosperous than he mistakenly believed they were. General Tilney, being an avaricious man himself and having observed the relationships developing between his two youngest children and Catherine Morland, decides to encourage a match between Henry and Catherine. When he discovers that he has been misinformed of the Morland family wealth, he blames Catherine. She has never represented herself as anything other than what she is, but in his rage over being deceived, General Tilney does not care.

Henry, learning the story from his father, refuses to abandon Catherine. The relationship that his father had encouraged has flourished, and Henry considers himself obligated by circumstances as well as by heartfelt emotion to marry Catherine. He tells his father so before leaving for Fullerton.

Catherine agrees to marry Henry, providing he gets her parents' approval. They are surprised by the attachment, but see no harm in Henry. The one condition they make is that Henry must have his father's approval before the marriage can take place. Their principles require that "while his parent so expressly forbad the connexion, they could not allow themselves to encourage it" (204). They do not require that General Tilney ever desire the marriage or provide additional income to Henry on the basis of it, but they do insist that the General give at least the "appearance of consent" to the union (204).

Henry returns to Woodston, and Catherine stays at Fullerton. They are committed to each other but have no idea how long they may have to wait to marry. In the meantime, another marriage takes place. Eleanor Tilney has, it seems, been in love for many years with a gentleman who was her inferior socially. They had been excessively discreet about their relationship, knowing that the General would be furious to think of his daughter in love with a man her inferior socially and economically. But Eleanor's suitor suddenly receives an "unexpected accession to title and fortune," which removes the only barrier to the General's approval. As a result, Eleanor marries a Viscount, and the newlyweds convince the General to accept Catherine as Henry's bride.

CHARACTER DEVELOPMENT

Scholars often discuss the detailed development of Jane Austen's characters. Her most significant characters in almost every novel are described and developed so finely that the reader often feels she or he knows them as well as anyone in daily life. Even relatively minor characters are often that clearly delineated. Austen herself, in the years after *Pride and Prejudice* was published, talked of seeing a portrait at an art exhibition that was the very image of Jane Bennet Bingley. And members of her family have revealed details about the lives of the characters beyond the end of the novels, details that she and her family created because, for them, the characters were as thoroughly alive as their friends and relatives.

The one Austen novel for which this level of characterization does not hold true is *Northanger Abbey*. The characters in this novel do not leap off the page and into imagination in the same way that Elizabeth Bennet, Captain Wentworth, and Emma Woodhouse do. Nor are they supposed to. In *Northanger*

Abbey, the characters are developed very differently than in Austen's other novels. They are less finely developed, which allows them to represent *types*, rather than carefully crafted individuals.

Austen's use of types rather than fully individualized characters in this novel allows her to focus the reader's attention directly on its commentary about books, forms of literature, and the action and consequences of reading instead of on getting to know the characters intimately. The character types she uses are those common to the literature of her day, types that would be easily recognizable by her contemporary audience.

Catherine Morland is the innocent young ingenue. For all of the narrator's claims that she is an unusual choice for a heroine, the essential qualities of the heroine are all present. Catherine has a good heart. She has difficulty, in fact, imagining that anyone she cares about could possibly behave badly on purpose. Despite obvious signs that Isabella is betraying James, Catherine believes that her friend is not conscious of her encouragement of Captain Tilney. She cannot allow herself to believe in such intentional wrong-doing on the part of her friend.

Catherine's innocence shows up in her own behavior as well. She never lies, always answering whatever questions she is asked as straightforwardly as possible. Others sometimes assume that she is answering coyly in order to be polite, for instance when General Tilney questions her about Mr. and Mrs. Allen's vast estate, but she doesn't know how to be coy. To be coy is to be disingenuous, and Catherine is absolutely genuine.

Catherine does, however, have an excitable imagination. Her reading has obviously included many gothic novels, and in her lack of experience of the world, she has accepted the world of the gothic as reality, not fantasy. As a result, she is easily led, first by Henry, then by her own mind, to imagine gothic horrors in the Abbey. A young girl with more experience of the world would recognize the distinction between fiction and reality more readily than Catherine does.

Catherine is the *type* of the heroine. In other words, she embodies the most fundamental qualities of the literary heroine of her time. Although not a beauty and not raised in difficult circumstances, she is young, innocent, and naïve. Her difficulties result primarily from the fact that she trusts people too much and is unable to discern truth from fiction, whether in the stories her friends tell or in the books she reads.

Henry Tilney, likewise, is a type of the hero. He is a self-sufficient individual who can and does stand on his own even in the face of great difficulties, in this case, the displeasure of his father. He loves the heroine because of her purity of spirit. He takes on the role of teacher to the woman he is growing to love when he begins to teach her about literature, art, and politics. He also instructs her in the difference between reality and fantasy when she allows her imagination to go too far. Many novels of Austen's time included heroes who took on the task of instructing their heroines, especially when the heroine was significantly younger, as is the case in *Northanger Abbey.*

While Henry is not a swashbuckling hero who must fight to the death Catherine's enemies, he does stand up for her, protect her to the best of his abilities, and ultimately provide her with the safety and security of a home filled with love and trust. Such is one common type of the eighteenth-century English hero.

Isabella and John Thorpe are also types. They represent the desperate fortune-hunters of both genders who pursue money to the exclusion of anything else. Qualities such as innocence and naïveté are only important to them in that they make their targets easier to con. The truth is meaningless to them; deception is their stock in trade. Loyalty is irrelevant; an engagement to one man or woman does not preclude the fortune-hunter from chasing an even larger fortune. Types like the Thorpe siblings can be found in many of the novels of Austen's time. In a social system in which one's status and opportunities were predicated on one's money, property, and title, fortune-hunters were omnipresent.

Mr. and Mrs. Allen also represent common types in literature. They represent the male and female varieties of good-natured, superficial, gentry-level society. Their thoughts and plans rarely move beyond what they will wear, which social event they will attend, and who they will talk with. Although they feel somewhat disturbed by Catherine's going out with her brother, Isabella, and John as much as she does, especially without adult female supervision, they never mention their concerns to her. This omission on their part does not result from a conscious decision to let her live life according to her own dictates; instead it comes from a superficiality that prevents them from thinking enough about the potential consequences of Catherine's actions to consider her behavior worth comment.

Mr. and Mrs. Allen are not bad people. They are, however, careless. Having taken charge of an innocent fifteen-year-old girl who has never been away from home before, they owe it to Catherine and her family to guide her behavior by word as well as deed. Their carelessness places her in danger of losing her good reputation and possibly even her innocence. Had John Thorpe been more interested in Catherine's person than in her father's bank account, he might very well have taken advantage of the young girl as they rode alone in the countryside outside Bath. The fact that Catherine survives with both her reputation and innocence intact is a credit to herself and fate, not to the Allens, the adults who are obligated to take care of the young woman.

Captain Tilney likewise is a specific character type. His is the type of the eldest son who believes that all the privileges in life should belong to him. He sees Isabella, is attracted to her, and goes after her, even after his brother tells him that she is engaged to another man. Captain Tilney is present only in a very small portion of the novel, but his wooing of Isabella from Catherine's brother James sets up the destruction of all hopes of marriage for the Morland siblings, albeit only temporarily in the case of Catherine and Henry.

Captain Tilney's type, the privilege-happy eldest son, usually creates hardship and destruction wherever he goes. In this novel the only permanent destruction is to the marital dreams of a deceitful fortune-hunter, which makes Frederick Tilney seem more an angel of mercy than a destroyer of dreams. But in most literature of Austen's time, this character type destroys the hopes and dreams of good people who are dependent upon him or his estate.

General Tilney fits the characteristics of a certain type of villain that was very common in the literature of eighteenth-century England. He is the harsh father/guardian figure who is more interested in increasing the money and power associated with his estate and position than he is in the happiness and care of his own children. Such a character, when carried to extremes in the gothic novel, is capable of murdering wives, kidnapping wealthy young heroines, and forcing his children into loveless marriages. When Catherine suspects General Tilney of the murder of his wife, she is reading his type correctly. In this novel he does not murder, but the harshness of his demeanor, the discomfort of his children when they are in his presence, the mercenary motives he displays when he believes Catherine to be wealthy, and his mistreatment of her when he discovers he has been misled are all characteristics of this particular type of villain in the literature of Austen's time.

THEMATIC ISSUES

One thematic concern in *Northanger Abbey* is parental responsibility. How much control is appropriate for a parent to have over offspring of marriageable age? How can and should a parent prepare a child to go out into the world and survive, preferably with morality intact? These questions are explored through several parents and parental figures in *Northanger Abbey*. Catherine Morland's parents demonstrate a trust in the honesty and innocence of their daughter that ignores the very real dangers a young girl with no knowledge of the world can face in a town like Bath. They do not prepare their daughter to recognize unscrupulous men and women who might take advantage of her, potentially endangering her reputation and even her life. They entrust her to the care of the Allens who are good friends of the family, but if they know the Allens well, they should realize that such guardians are not capable of the kind of discretion necessary to safely guide an innocent young girl through the maze of social activities available in a resort town like Bath.

The Allens stand in the place of parents for Catherine while she is in Bath. They do not, however, exert any control over her activities, allowing her to go where she wants, when she wants, with whom she wants. They act in this way not because Catherine would give them any trouble if they imposed rules but because they are simply careless. When Catherine herself mentions that she feels awkward about riding out alone with John Thorpe, the Allens agree that such carriage rides are not really appropriate. Catherine is disturbed that they haven't mentioned their views before. She would never have dreamt of behaving inappropriately, but the fact that Mr. and Mrs. Allen presented no objection of any kind when she had initially asked them for permission to go led her to believe that such an excursion was entirely appropriate. Catherine wants guidance. When she does not get it from the individuals who are placed in the position of parents, she finds herself having to rely on her own sense of right and wrong combined with the influence of the friends she meets in Bath. To allow a fifteen-year-old girl to parent herself in such a situation is the height of irresponsibility in adults who have been given the privilege and responsibility of acting in the place of her parents.

Mrs. Thorpe's parenting style is likewise problematic. She is a widow with four children and very little income. As a result, getting her children established in life is going to be difficult. But rather than preparing them to function in the world in respectable, albeit potentially low, positions, she encourages them to pursue marriage for money. Propriety, decorum, and morality are all qualities that she believes can be sacrificed when a profitable marriage could be the result. Thus, John Thorpe pursues Catherine, mistakenly believing her to be rich. When he realizes his mistake, he destroys her reputation with General Tilney, an action that almost ruins her chance for happiness. Isabella seduces James Morland into an engagement with her only to desert him when a more profitable potential marriage partner comes along. Within the scope of the novel, neither of the Thorpes are successful at arranging a profitable marriage for themselves. Mrs. Thorpe's training them in the mercenary art of seduction does not, in fact, yield them the wealth, power, and position they anticipate.

General Tilney is another example of a poor parent. He, like Mrs. Thorpe, is a mercenary parent, insisting that his children marry for money and position. Whether they also love their mates is, to him, irrelevant. Unlike Mrs. Thorpe, however, General Tilney's mercenary actions are not born out of financial desperation. He is motivated by pride and greed. His own marriage seems not to have been built on the basis of love or affection, and he appears to have no understanding that a marriage based on those qualities could be more advantageous to the individuals involved than one based on financial considerations.

General Tilney's insistence on his children marrying wealth is, however, only one of his faults as a parent. His rigidity and lack of warmth also create difficulties. He runs his home like a military operation, everything following a firm time schedule, no matter whether circumstances warrant or not. Catherine is first exposed to this rigidity on the day she arrives at Northanger Abbey. Despite the fact that the family has just completed a long journey, no leeway is allowed in the hour of dinner. At five on the dot, dinner must be on the table and all members of the household must be in their places to sit down to it.

General Tilney's rigidity combines with his mercenary streak when he learns that his son, Henry, is determined to marry Catherine despite the fact she does not have the wealth the General requires of his children's mates. General Tilney, having forbidden his son even to "think" of her anymore, is horrified when his son disobeys (199). Henry not only thinks of Catherine, he proposes to her and refuses to return to his father's house until she can return with him as his wife. General Tilney finally relents, but only after his new son-in-law, a Viscount, convinces him to do so.

General Tilney's lack of warmth and emotional support for his children creates an environment in the home in which tension is the customary state. Catherine's gothic imaginings of General Tilney as the murderer of his wife are proven to be mistaken, but his coldness does have the effect of killing any positive displays of emotion at Northanger except when the General is absent. He appears to have no interest in the hopes and dreams of his children, only in his own plans for their futures. The result is the creation of a home that everyone wants to leave. Frederick Tilney rarely visits his father's house, and Henry, though present frequently, explains that his reason for being there is to support his sister, Eleanor, who has no choice but to live in the cold, joyless Abbey with her father. When Henry's decision to disobey his father and engage himself to Catherine despite his father's wishes causes him to avoid the Abbey, his only concern is that he cannot be as available for Eleanor.

In addition to presenting a critique of poor parenting, *Northanger Abbey* offers a commentary on the education of the young adult in the ways of the world. Catherine Morland begins the novel as a young girl, very innocent and quite naïve. Upon her arrival in Bath, she finds a world filled with different kinds of people and a variety of activities that would never have been available to her in the countryside with her family. In Bath she must quickly learn to be discerning if she is to become experienced in the ways of the world without losing her essential innocence.

Catherine's first teachers in Bath are the Thorpes. They provide her with experiences she has never had, including the attentions of an attractive young man. Although in her naïveté she does not recognize the deceit and harmful intentions in Isabella and John's manipulations, Catherine does feel uncomfortable with many of their words and actions. Her essential goodness is well enough developed that she intuitively knows something is wrong. Nonetheless, she is fortunate to escape her contact with them with her reputation and innocence intact.

Henry Tilney and his sister Eleanor are her next pair of teachers. They, fortunately, are young people with good morals and much experience of the world. Catherine is drawn to their goodness, as well as to Henry as an attractive man who has been attentive to her.

The first mode of education the Tilneys supply Catherine with is that of modeling appropriate behavior. As her dancing partner, Henry behaves well towards Catherine. He is attentive to her, converses with her about topics she finds both interesting and amusing, and leads her easily and comfortably around the dance floor. He demonstrates the courtesy that she should expect of a partner, a courtesy that John Thorpe sorely lacks.

Eleanor likewise models proper behavior for Catherine. She talks with Catherine on appropriate topics, never gossiping or manipulating like Isabella Thorpe. Towards her father she always shows respect and obedience, even when his treatment of her leaves much to be desired. When Henry and Eleanor go out for a walk with Catherine, the walk remains completely proper, with the two young women always together, preventing any possibility of the reputation of either woman being sullied by being placed in an inappropriate situation with a man.

When walking with Henry and Eleanor at Beechen Cliff, Catherine expresses her opinion that Henry undoubtedly does not read novels. She makes this assumption on the basis of the fact that she has heard men like John Thorpe discuss novels in degrading terms, leading her to believe that "gentlemen read better books" (83). Henry responds with a strong endorsement of novels: "The person, be it gentleman or lady, who has not pleasure in a good novel, must be intolerably stupid. I have read all Mrs. Radcliffe's works, and most of them with great pleasure" (83). In fact, Henry claims, "If we proceed to particulars, and engage in the never-ceasing inquiry of 'Have you read this?' and 'Have you read that?' I shall soon leave you . . . far behind me" (84). Novels, Henry explains to Catherine, can provide hours of pleasure to the reader. In addition, they can provide the individual with a kind of vicarious experience of life that can add to a person's store of knowledge about people and the world.

Catherine then discusses her personal dislike of reading history. History is, she claims, the "quarrels of popes and kings, with wars or pestilences, in every page; the men all so good for nothing, and hardly any women at all—it is very tiresome" (85). Eleanor explains that she, in fact, likes history very much. She enjoys learning the truth about the past and enjoys reading the words of men like Mr. Hume and Mr. Robertson (two of the premiere historians of the day) which are so well crafted. Catherine is not won over, but she does acknowledge that Eleanor's enjoyment of history, together with the fact that her father, Mr. Allen, and two of her brothers are also fans of historical writing, makes her question her assumption that historical writing is necessarily dry and boring.

Eleanor and Henry then begin admiring the countryside "with the eyes of persons accustomed to drawing . . . with all the eagerness of real taste" (86). Catherine listens intently to their discussion but has nothing to contribute since she knows "nothing of drawing—nothing of taste" (86). They talked of "fore-grounds, distances, and second distances—side-screens and perspectives—lights and shades" (87). Catherine soaks up all the knowledge she can from their conversation. She learns that there is much more to painting and drawing than merely creating a realistic representation of an attractive view.

Their conversation continues, covering topics as varied as Romanticism, land usage laws, the crown, the government, and politics. Each topic is a new area of intellectual thought for Catherine, exposing her to new ideas and new ways of thinking. Henry and Eleanor Tilney are worldly young people in that they are aware of and keep themselves informed about what is happening in the world around them. They, unlike the Thorpes, do not restrict their interests to social events and mercenary marital plans. From the Tilneys, Catherine learns to think, not merely to react.

Catherine's education is not complete by the end of the novel, but in the course of her visits to Bath and Northanger Abbey, she learns when to trust or distrust her intuition. She also learns that she can think intellectually about a number of subjects and that, if she has good guides, she can learn much that is useful and enjoyable from books and conversation as well as from the experiences life sends her.

A METAFICTIONAL READING OF *NORTHANGER ABBEY*

A work of fiction in which one of the major concerns is the nature of fiction itself is called a metafiction. Modern novels such as John Fowles's *The French Lieutenant's Woman* are often discussed in terms of metafiction because of their multiple narrative perspectives, but the metafictional approach is rarely applied to literature written prior to the twentieth century. Approaching *Northanger Abbey* as a work of metafiction, however, is extremely productive because it is a novel in which Austen explores the methods and purposes customary for novelists of her time. Thus, it explores the literary milieu in which she both lives and writes. Her exploration is both overt and subtle, sometimes allowing the narrator to speak directly to the reader about literature, sometimes indirectly addressing literary issues through the structure of the novel and commentary by characters within the novel itself.

Northanger Abbey opens with a direct discussion of Catherine Morland as a heroine. Rather than immediately immersing the reader into a realistic setting and fully developed characters from the very beginning, the reader is reminded, over and over, that the book he or she holds is a novel, a work of fiction, not to be confused with reality. The contrast between Catherine's background and that of the traditional heroine is made clear, but while such a contrast allows Catherine to stand out among heroines, it also causes the reader to focus on her as a literary type, not a realistic individual.

Catherine's tendency to expect to find the trappings of gothic literature everywhere she looks at Northanger Abbey is ridiculed by Henry Tilney and even by the reader as we recognize her book-influenced imagination at work. But the serious issues at the heart of the gothic novel, issues that include the dangers of women's complete dependence on men and the reality that evil exists in the world, sometimes in the very people the innocent most depend upon, are treated quite seriously. The gothic novel may indeed contain exaggerations in its accouterments, as *Northanger Abbey* freely acknowledges, but at its core, Austen's novel indicates, gothic novels explore serious issues about life and human nature.

Austen even includes an explicit defense of the novel in *Northanger Abbey*. Having mentioned that Catherine and Isabella read novels together, the narrator launches into what may be one of the most energetic defenses of novel reading ever written. "Yes, novels," the narrator insists:

for I will not adopt that ungenerous and impolitic custom so common with novel writers, of degrading by their contemptuous censure the very performances, to the number of which they are themselves adding—joining with their greatest enemies in bestowing the harshest epithets on such works, and scarcely ever permitting them to be read by their own heroine, who, if she accidentally takes up a novel, is sure to turn over its insipid pages with disgust. Alas! if the heroine of one novel be not patronized by the heroine of another, from whom can she expect protection and regard? . . . Let us not desert one another. . . . Although our productions have afforded more extensive and unaffected pleasure than those of any other literary corporation in the world, no species of composition has been so much decried. . . . "Oh! it is only a novel!" replies the young lady, while she lays down her book with affected indifference, or momentary shame.—"it is only Cecilia, or Camilla, or Belinda"; or, in short, only some work in which the greatest powers of the mind are displayed, in which the most thorough knowledge of human nature, the happiest delineation of its varieties, the liveliest effusions of wit and humour are conveyed to the world in the best chosen language. (21–22)

The movement of this passage is followed by the events of the novel itself. Catherine, as a heroine of a novel, reads novels. She initially believes, however, that others, more intelligent than she is, will read "better books" (83). She is disabused of that idea by Henry, who insists on the novel's capacity for providing enjoyment. But the novel, like the narrator's defense of the genre, goes much further in claiming social, emotional, and ethical significance for the genre, demonstrating through realistic depictions of characters and events that the novel, at its best, displays "the greatest power of the mind," "the most thorough knowledge of human nature," and "the liveliest effusions of wit and humour" that can be "conveyed to the world in the best chosen language" (23). By exploring a wide range of novelistic devices and concerns in *Northanger Abbey*, Austen claims rightful access to the full range of the genre's possibilities. As a result, she carves out a place for herself and her novels, positioning herself in relation to her contemporaries and predecessors. For Austen, a novel is never "just a novel." It may be good or bad; it may succeed or fail, just like other literary forms. In using *Northanger Abbey* as a form of metafiction, Austen treats the genre of the novel as the equal of any other literary form. She also creates and defines a niche for herself among the talented and important group of writers known as novelists.

8

Persuasion
(1818)

At the time of her death, Jane Austen left behind a manuscript of the novel that came to be known as *Persuasion*. She had not yet titled the work, nor had she completed revisions of it. Nonetheless, as a result of the continued interest in the author and her work, her family decided to publish the novel posthumously.

Persuasion differs significantly from her earlier novels. The heroine, Anne Elliot, is older, past the first bloom of life. She is also a member of the aristocracy, albeit a younger daughter of a baronet who is strapped for funds and who does not travel in the highest of social circles. But even more significant than the difference in her heroine is the difference in her hero. Captain Wentworth is a navy captain. His family, unlike those of Austen's earlier heroes, does not own property. His brother is a clergyman, and his sister is married to a fellow navy man, Admiral Croft.

In Austen's final novel, the importance of earning one's own place in the world is much more significant than in the earlier novels. All of the admirable male characters in *Persuasion* are self-made naval men, representing the new nineteenth-century concept of meritorious conduct over situation of birth. Admiral Croft, Captain Wentworth, Captain Harville, and Captain Benwick all are discussed in terms of their meritorious activity in the war. Their fortunes are won in battle and their place in society is determined, in large part, by those actions. The old ways of establishing one's place through inheritance and patronage is represented most strongly by the Elliot men, Sir Walter Elliot and his heir apparent, William Walter Elliot. These men concern themselves with issues of wealth and social precedence rather than useful activity. They are portrayed as vain and egotistical, more concerned with appearance (both physical beauty and how things appear to others) than with activity.

Along with the change from a world based predominantly on inheritance and patronage to one in which merit can earn its due comes a change in the tone of the novel. *Persuasion* is a novel filled with activity. It is not as sentimental about eighteenth-century English country life as Austen's other novels. Instead, it focuses on a future in which self-made professional men, instead of the few gentlemen who inherit lands and titles, will control English society and commerce. Jane Austen, with three brothers in the navy (two of whom achieve the status of Admiral before they retire), recognized the role that men of action could play in the future of the nation. She never lost sight of the importance of inherited property—her brother Edward's fortune was a direct result of his being adopted by an aunt and uncle so that they would have an heir to their estate—but, in *Persuasion*, she pays homage to the active self-made man, a phenomenon that would become more and more important as the nineteenth century progressed.

PLOT SUMMARY

The novel opens over eight years after Anne Elliot and young Wentworth met and fell in love. We learn in the course of the novel that their love was strong and true, and that Anne was prepared to marry Wentworth even though he did not have a sufficient income to support a wife at the time he proposed. She turned down his offer of marriage, however, when Lady Russell, a close friend of Anne's late mother and Anne's moral guide and mentor throughout her teenage and early adult years, persuaded her to give up the attachment. Lady Russell believed such an engagement to be extremely imprudent and felt it her duty to prevent Anne from making a mistake in attaching herself to an impoverished young man.

When the novel opens, Anne is twenty-seven years old and well past the bloom of early womanhood. We learn that, when she was younger, she had at least two suitors: Wentworth, whom she was and continues to be deeply in love with, and Charles Hayter, a local man who will eventually inherit a small estate in the same neighborhood as her father's. She rejected both, the first because of the influence of Lady Russell and the second because she did not love him.

Anne lives with her father, Sir Walter Elliot, and her oldest sister, Elizabeth, at the family estate of Kellynch. Anne is the most sensible and practical individual in the household, but her advice is rarely asked for and never followed. In fact, her presence is merely tolerated. Sir Walter and Elizabeth are excessively proud of their position in the community. Their pride is based not on actions and abilities, but on titles, property, and personal appearance. Anne, as a younger daughter in a world where elder daughters always take precedence and a woman who has lost the bloom of youthful beauty, holds a position of no importance in the Elliot family—at least according to her father and sister. Her practical approach to life is antithetical to their sense of entitlement, and her fading beauty prevents her from being appreciated as a decorative ornament for the family.

We soon learn that Sir Walter has not been a careful manager of his estate and income. In fact, he can no longer afford to live at Kellynch without giving up most of the pleasures that generally accompany life on a country estate. His options are either to retrench in place, requiring a substantial reduction in his standard of living, or to rent Kellynch to someone with money to spare and move himself and his family to less expensive quarters. Sir Walter, with the assistance of his business manager and Lady Russell, concludes that the latter choice will discomfit him the least. As soon as his business manager finds a suitable tenant for Kellynch, the Elliots arrange to leave for Bath.

As usual, Anne's desires and interests are not consulted in the decision to move or retrench in place. Her father, Elizabeth, and a good friend of Elizabeth's, the young widow Mrs. Clay, head for Bath to find lodgings that will enable them to spend significantly less money while retaining the appearance of wealth and social standing. Anne, disliking Bath intensely from her time in school there, remains behind to assist her younger sister, Mary, nurse one of her children through the aftermath of an injury due to a fall. The plan is that she will join her father and sister in Bath once they have comfortably settled themselves.

The tenants Mr. Shepherd finds to rent Kellynch are Admiral and Mrs. Croft. They are strong individuals with considerable wealth won by the Admiral in the recently ended war with France. Mrs. Croft is the former Miss Wentworth, sister to Captain Wentworth, Anne Elliot's great love. The Crofts are unaware, however, of the former relationship between Captain Wentworth and Anne.

Anne is pleased to be staying with her sister Mary Musgrove rather than with Lady Russell while her father and sister find a place to settle in Bath. With Lady Russell's home so close to Kellynch, it would be virtually impossible for her to avoid seeing them on a regular basis if she were living there. She prefers to avoid the danger of hearing too much about Captain Wentworth or, even worse, being forced to run into him when he visits his sister at Kellynch. By staying with Mary, even though it is only a few miles from Kellynch, Anne believes that she will avoid the likelihood of running into Captain Wentworth.

When Captain Wentworth visits his sister at Kellynch, he becomes acquainted with Mary Musgrove's sisters-in-law, Henrietta and Louisa, and he begins visiting the Musgroves frequently. Anne finds herself forced to see him when he visits. Such frequent interactions with the man she refused to marry eight years before are extremely uncomfortable for her, especially since she discovers he is still the only man she can imagine sharing a life with.

Captain Wentworth behaves civilly towards Anne Elliot, but civility is the extent of their interaction throughout most of the novel. Both of the unmarried Musgrove girls being attracted to the handsome naval officer, they vie for his attentions on each and every visit. Anne finds herself having to watch as Captain Wentworth flirts with both young women.

Upon discovering that a couple of very good men who had served under him were living in the resort town of Lyme, Captain Wentworth decides to visit them. He mentions his plans to the Musgroves, and they decide to make an overnight party of it. Henrietta, Louisa, Mary, Charles (her husband), and Anne are all included.

While in Lyme, the entire company, accompanied by Captain Benwick, a friend and former subordinate of Captain Wentworth, goes for a walk by the seaside. At one point where they must climb down some wooden stairs, Louisa decides to jump down from the top, with Captain Wentworth to catch her and keep her from falling. Despite warnings of the danger involved, she successfully makes the jump. Having enjoyed the thrill of it, she races back up the stairs in order to repeat the experience. The second time is not successful. She falls and is knocked unconscious.

In the confusion that follows, Anne takes control of the situation. When Captain Wentworth begins to run off in search of a doctor, Anne stops him, insisting that Captain Benwick is the more appropriate man to send since he better knows the town and its residents. She calms her sister Mary and begins making arrangements to carry Louisa back to town.

When Captain Benwick returns, he has instructions to bring Louisa to Captain Harville's home where she can be looked after by Mrs. Harville. The doctor, he tells them, will meet them there. The entire company go to the Harville's. Louisa remains unconscious and develops a fever. News is sent to Louisa's parents of the accident, and they make arrangements to come as soon as they can.

Ultimately it is decided that Louisa can best recover in Lyme, that moving her home would not be in her best interest. Captain Wentworth feels responsible for the accident, believing that he should have been able to convince Louisa not to risk a fall, regardless of her headstrong desire to leap into his arms. He makes certain that she is being well cared for, but he spends little time with her during her convalescence in Lyme, in part because his temperament is not conducive to the requirements of nursing but also because, in the aftermath of the accident, he has discovered that most of Louisa's family is certain of a more serious attachment between them than he has intended. Once he realizes that he may have led Louisa to believe he is interested in marrying her, he considers himself obligated to do so when she recovers. He hopes, however, that some distance between them will diminish her interest in him and that, by the time she has recovered, the attachment will be reduced in her mind to nothing more than an innocent flirtation.

In Captain Wentworth's absence, Captain Benwick takes over as Louisa's companion and protector. Captain Benwick is a very sensitive man. He had previously been engaged to Captain Harville's sister, Fanny, but while he was out on the high seas earning sufficient wealth to enable them to marry, Fanny Harville became very ill and died. At the time of the Musgrove party's visit to Lyme, Fanny had been dead for only seven months. Captain Benwick had always been a rather quiet and bookish man (though no less an effective sailor as a result), but Fanny's death causes him to become even more introverted, more depressed, and more involved in reading poetry of love and loss than he had been before. Captain Benwick's quiet ways suit the sickroom well, and Louisa's health improves as he administers to her needs in the Harville household.

Louisa's accident results in a permanent change in her high spirits and reckless behavior. She becomes a much quieter, more serious young woman. Her taste in literature and philosophy has been permanently changed by her exposure during her recovery to the ideas and poetry most admired by Captain Benwick. By the time she has fully recovered, she and Captain Benwick have fallen deeply in love.

Captain Wentworth, therefore, avoids being permanently attached to Louisa Musgrove, a woman he never had serious intentions towards. He recognizes and appreciates his escape from such a marriage. He realizes that, despite having mild flirtations with a number of women in the years since Anne Elliot broke his heart, he has never met any other woman who could tempt him to marry.

Meanwhile, Sir Walter and Elizabeth have completed their task of finding, renting, and furnishing lodgings for the family in Bath, and Anne has been taken to live with them by Lady Russell, who has taken lodgings of her own in Bath. Both Anne and Lady Russell are concerned when they find that there are no plans to send Mrs. Clay away upon Anne's joining the party. Their concern is based on the fact that Mrs. Clay seems to be trying to insinuate herself into Sir Walter's life in such a way as to persuade him to marry her. That Sir Walter could marry again at all is a distressing matter to his heir apparent, William Elliot, since it means that Sir Walter could yet have a son who would usurp the cousin's hereditary position. But that he might marry Mrs. Clay is a fact that disturbs far more people since Mrs. Clay is a manipulative woman of common birth whose first priority is to find a good provider for her future. Both Anne and Lady Russell abhor the thought that Mrs. Clay might take the place of the gracious and benevolent woman who had been Anne, Elizabeth, and Mary's mother.

Mr. William Elliot, the heir apparent to Sir Walter's title and estate, introduces himself to the family while they are in Bath. William's father had had a falling-out with Sir Walter many years past, and the families have not communicated for a very long time. But the younger Mr. Elliot, upon discovering that the present owner of Kellynch is in Bath, arranges an introduction for himself and begins to ingratiate himself into the family. He, unlike Sir Walter, has sufficient funds to support an aristocratic lifestyle, having been married to a woman of great wealth though of low family connections. His wife died less than a year before the novel begins, and Mr. Elliot is still dressed in mourning, though he does not appear to feel any grief. In fact, his primary interest appears to be courting his cousin Anne.

Anne is interested in developing a civil acquaintance with her cousin, but she is not interested in him romantically. She recognizes how pleasing he makes himself to her, but she is perceptive enough to realize that he manages to make himself equally pleasing to everyone connected with her family—even those whom he speaks disapprovingly of to her. She doubts the authenticity of the feelings he expresses and suggests to Lady Russell, who admires him greatly, that there is something improper about him, although she cannot quite explain what it is.

Anne behaves quite properly with Mr. Elliot. Having only a feeling that all is not right in his motivations and behavior, she does not accuse him of any particular indiscretion. Also, since he is a member of the family and is invited to many family activities by her father and sister, she feels it necessary to treat him as befits a member of the family. When Mr. Elliot treats her with a degree of intimacy that could be viewed as a precursor to courtship, she overlooks it, not knowing for certain what his intentions are towards her and not wanting to assume a desire for a closer relationship than he is actually anticipating.

Captain Wentworth comes to Bath with his friend Captain Harville. While in Bath, Wentworth closely observes Anne, particularly the interactions between Anne and Mr. Elliot. He determines that Mr. Elliot is, indeed, courting Anne, and that her responses to him are such as may indicate a willingness on her part to be courted by him. Anne's first indication that Captain Wentworth may still have deep feelings for her is his apparent jealousy over Mr. Elliot's closeness to her. Until that point, she is certain that her refusal of his proposal eight years previously had ended any chance for them to have a future together.

The jealousy, however, allows Anne to hope that his love for her has not died in the intervening years.

While in Bath, Anne visits Mrs. Smith, an impoverished widow who was a good friend of hers years before at school. Mrs. Smith, though an invalid who rarely leaves her rooms, is very knowledgeable about everything happening in Bath. A good friend of hers is Nurse Rooke, who works for various members of the social elite in Bath. Through her interactions with people from all walks of life, Nurse Rooke learns all the gossip of Bath and brings it to her friend, Mrs. Smith, as a means of entertaining the poor, young invalid. Thus, Mrs. Smith knows much more than Anne tells her about the activities in the Elliot household. She hears about Mr. Elliot's attentions to Anne and is the first to inform Anne of Mr. Elliot's intention to propose marriage to her.

Upon Anne's assurance that she has no intention of ever marrying her cousin, Mrs. Smith decides that she should inform Anne of Mr. Elliot's less admirable side. Through Mrs. Smith, therefore, Anne discovers that Mr. Elliot has a very questionable history. He married his first wife exclusively for her money and mistreated her throughout their marriage. He also speculates, investing money in shaky deals and encouraging his friends, many of whom do not have his financial resources, to do the same. It is through one of these investment schemes that Mrs. Smith's husband lost his money. Soon after, he died, leaving his wife ill and in debt. Mr. Smith had named Mr. Elliot as the executor of his will, but regardless of how often and desperately Mrs. Smith contacts him asking for help disentangling the confusion of the financial situation she faces, Mr. Elliot ignores her. Mrs. Smith is sufficiently aware of her husband's financial situation to realize that there is one asset that, if handled properly, could ease her situation considerably. It is a property she owns in America. In her current state of health and finances, she cannot make the trip to America herself nor does she have the means to hire someone to make it for her. She has requested, time after time, that Mr. Elliot look into this property for her but has never received a response.

Mrs. Smith also has it on good authority that Mr. Elliot reconciled with Sir Walter's branch of the Elliot family initially because he heard that Mrs. Clay had her sights set on Sir Walter. Not wanting to lose the title or the estate of Kellynch, both of which he has long considered to be rightfully his, he arranged to be introduced into the family in order to prevent Mrs. Clay, by any means possible, from convincing Sir Walter to marry her. At the very time he is courting Anne, he is also meeting clandestinely with Mrs. Clay. He has no intention, of course, of marrying the young widow. His motivation is to prevent her marrying Sir Walter and producing a son who would stand between him and the title he desperately wants.

At the end of the novel, Anne Elliot and Captain Wentworth finally come to understand each other. Anne recognizes that Captain Wentworth still cares about her, but his pride prevents him from approaching her in a manner that allows her to maintain her sense of propriety and decorum while acknowledging that she still loves him as much as she ever has. The opportunity finally arrives for such mutual understanding when Captain Wentworth and Captain Harville visit the Musgroves one day in Bath. Captain Harville talks privately with Anne, who is also present, about his friend Captain Benwick's engagement to Louisa Musgrove. He expresses his view that Captain Benwick's grief over Fanny Harville's death seems to have been too short-lived if the captain can have fallen in love again so fast. Anne sympathizes with him, but explains that her experience has shown her that men, due in large part to their greater activity in the world, tend not to feel such pain as deeply or as long as women do. Women, Anne suggests, rarely forget men as quickly as men forget them:

It is, perhaps, our fate rather than our merit. We cannot help ourselves. We live at home, quiet, confined, and our feelings prey upon us. You [men] are forced on exertion. You have always a profession, pursuits, business of some sort or other, to take you back to the world immediately, and continual occupation and change soon weaken impressions. (198)

Captain Harville does not want to grant that Captain Benwick has been as loyal and constant to Fanny Harville's memory as can be expected of a man, but he has to admit that Anne has a point. And the fact that Anne seems to be speaking directly from her heart, indicating that she has personally experienced the kind of pain she is discussing, makes her argument quite powerful.

Captain Harville is not the only person in the room to hear her remarks. Captain Wentworth, who is sitting at a desk writing a letter, overhears. In her words he recognizes a depth of feeling and a degree of constancy that he has not previously given her credit for. After completing the letter he is writing, he takes another sheet of paper and drafts a letter to Anne, asking if there is still a chance for them. He leaves it with her when he and Captain Harville take their leave. When she reads it, she comes close to losing control. To have the happiness she thought lost forever so close is almost too much to bear. She quickly leaves the Musgroves and heads home. Along the way she runs into Captain Wentworth (by design rather than accident), and they finally talk openly about their past and potential future. By the end of their conversation, they renew their engagement, knowing that this time Anne's family and friends can have no legitimate opposition to the marriage on the basis of finances. They also know that Anne would not succumb to any persuasion against the marriage now that she is a mature woman of twenty-seven instead of an innocent and easily-influenced young girl of nineteen.

Anne's family and friends have no objection to the marriage: it provides for Anne's future without placing her above either of her sisters socially. Captain Wentworth's family is thrilled to have Anne among them. The Crofts admire and appreciate her long before her relationship with Captain Wentworth is known. Reverend Wentworth, the Captain's brother, has also known and respected Anne for many years. As a Wentworth, Anne will be appreciated for her true values rather than deprecated for her fading beauty and lack of concern about the intricate complexities of social position among the owners of property in England.

CHARACTER DEVELOPMENT

The novel *Persuasion* is poised on the boundary between traditional eighteenth-century English literature and the literature of the English Romantics. It, more than any other of Jane Austen's novels, illustrates the differing mindsets between those who choose to maintain the traditions of eighteenth-century England and those who choose to change with the times. Austen's character development in *Persuasion* focuses on the differences between these approaches. Characters who choose to retain the old ways are depicted as relatively static characters who do not change over time. Characters whose lives support the changes that accompany Romanticism, with its focus on originality and independence of thought and action, are dynamic characters, changing through time as they continue to learn and grow. Neither side is depicted as being exclusively right or wrong: errors in judgment can and do occur on both sides. But the necessity to change with the changing world in the second decade of the nineteenth century causes those characters with the desire, energy, and ability to change with the times to be more successful, overall, than those concerned only with maintaining the status quo.

Heading the list of the characters whose lives depend upon the maintenance of tradition is Sir Walter Elliot. Sir Walter epitomizes those in England whose land and titles were earned many generations in the past and who, by the late eighteenth century, have degenerated into idle holders of property, interested only in their entitlements and privileges, caring nothing about the responsibilities that had been expected of the aristocracy in previous generations. Sir Walter is concerned about the appearance of his person and the prestige given him by his estate and title. Nothing else truly matters to him.

Sir Walter's oldest daughter, Elizabeth, is likewise a supporter of tradition. She relishes her position as the first daughter of a widowed baronet. That position allows her to act as hostess for her father and to take credit for running his household. It enables her to act as mistress of the house from a very young age and without the disadvantages that could result from marrying a man who might not allow her the freedom her father does. Like her father, Elizabeth cherishes beauty and position. She is quite beautiful herself and believes she is entitled to everyone's attention as a result of her beauty and social position. For both Elizabeth and her father, the *Baronetage* is the book most read. It is a book that focuses entirely on defining one's social position, lineage, and prestige—exclusively by bloodline. It is, in a sense, the bible of social position and lineage. By turning so frequently to the entry of their own family, as well as by examining the *Baronetage* for the lineage of those individuals with whom they come in contact, Sir Walter and his eldest daughter reinforce the image of themselves as creatures of superficiality, having no personal or ethical depth. Their bible is not a book espousing morality, spirituality, and philosophy. Instead it is a book that reveals only the surface connections of bloodlines and property ownership.

Lady Russell is a crossover character between those whose allegiances are with tradition and those who admire the new Romantic ideals. She has a very strong vested interest in maintaining the status quo, having attained her social position, wealth, and power through it. She is capable, however, of learning to appreciate certain of the qualities that accompany the onset of Romanticism. In particular, she admires those who have managed to build successful lives based on their own individual merit. When Captain Wentworth first applied for Anne Elliot's hand in marriage, Lady Russell strongly opposed the idea, persuading Anne to refuse him because he did not have sufficient income to provide a home suitable for the daughter of a baronet. Eight years later, however, after he has earned a significant fortune from successful naval campaigns to support Anne in a style Lady Russell considers appropriate for a woman of her social standing, she approves the marriage. The difference those eight years have made is essential. In those years, Captain Wentworth has grown from an ambitious young man with much energy but no guaranteed assets into a more mature, successful naval captain with a substantial bank account. He is no longer a young man who merely has the potential to do well; he is a man who has proven himself worthy. Lady Russell, unlike Sir Walter, is not stuck in the notion that lineage and family estates are necessarily superior to earning one's way through meritorious conduct. A gentleman who has earned his own substantial fortune through his own efforts is, for her, worthy of marrying a woman of Anne Elliot's social standing and exceptional character.

The age of Romanticism, with its focus on individuality, originality, and success through individual meritorious conduct, is best represented in the novel through the Navy. Admiral and Mrs. Croft, Captain and Mrs. Harville, Captain Benwick, and Captain Wentworth all represent aspects of Romanticism, a more dynamic and forward-looking philosophy of life than that which ruled throughout most of the eighteenth century in England.

Admiral and Mrs. Croft are the first characters we meet in the novel whose lives run counter to traditional eighteenth-century expectations. Admiral Croft is a self-made man. Although he may have entered the navy and gained some early promotion through the patronage of powerful men of property in England (as did most naval officers of the time), his advancement to the rank of admiral and the fortune he amassed as bounty for the ships he has captured at sea, have resulted from his own meritorious activity. The "self-made man" is a term that did not come into vogue until later in the nineteenth century under the reign of Queen Victoria, but the concept of a man rising in both social standing and fortune as a result of his own activity was a concept gaining ground in England by the later years of Austen's life. Admiral Croft and the Captains of the British Navy in *Persuasion* represent that concept quite commendably.

Mrs. Croft is the only thoroughly modern woman in *Persuasion*. She is an active force in the novel—substantially more active than any other woman. She is a unique character among Austen's fictional women in that she is truly her husband's equal, not only in social position and moral sensibilities, but also in her opinions and activities. Mrs. Croft has traveled on shipboard throughout most of her husband's career. She is a good sailor, a good coachwoman, and a good companion to her husband; she braves dangers by his side as thoroughly as she shares the fruits of his labor. Mrs. Croft is instrumental in the business of settling the terms of their tenancy at Kellynch. In fact, she determines more of the specific terms of their lease than her husband, demonstrating, in the process, her fine head for business and her expectation that she will be treated as the equal of her husband even in activities most people of her time consider exclusively within the masculine domain.

Austen has placed Mrs. Croft in circumstances which best allow her to shine as a modern woman. She and Admiral Croft have no children; therefore she is never relegated to the nursery or indisposed due to pregnancy or childbirth. Her husband's income is sufficient to prevent her from having to be a household drudge like Mrs. Price in *Mansfield Park*. Her husband is a modern man who neither expects nor wants her to fit into the role of a conventional wife. As a result, she is able to act freely, in accordance with her nature, instead of having to fit her personality into preexisting expectations, no matter how poor the fit.

Captain Benwick, like his naval companions, is committed to succeeding on his own merits. But he represents another aspect of Romanticism as well: the indulgence of emotion in both life and literature. When we first meet Captain Benwick, he is in mourning for Fanny Harville, the woman he was engaged to marry. Captain Benwick, predisposed by nature towards solitude and intense feelings, grieves deeply for his lost love. Instead of finding activity that might assist him in overcoming his grief, he indulges it, reading Romantic poetry about lost love and characters destined for lonely, solitary lives. The intensity of Captain Benwick's grief and his tendency to indulge it worries his friends who fear that he might drive himself into complete despair, possibly resulting in madness or death. Thus, Captain Benwick represents Romantic sensibilities not only as a man who has achieved success on his own merits but also as a reader of Romantic literature and as one who enjoys the world of the Romantic: wild and uncontrollable Nature existing in the inner reality of the individual as well as in the outer world.

Captain Wentworth and Anne Elliot together represent the best of the new Romantics in combination with the best of English tradition. His ambition combines with her lineage, his activity with her thoughtfulness, his determination with her moral rectitude. Together they represent the best while leaving behind those aspects of tradition which are degenerating as well as the unhealthy extremes of the new Romanticism.

Captain Wentworth was born into a respectable family. His brother is a rector and his sister the wife of an Admiral. Although his parents' background is not specified in the course of the novel, they were probably of lower gentry status and did not own a significant amount of property. Captain Wentworth is, therefore, the son of a gentleman. As such, his family's status is not so low that he cannot ever expect to be an eligible mate for Anne Elliot, the daughter of a baronet who outspends his income. But his eligibility is predicated on his being able to support her appropriately. If Captain Wentworth had not had the ambition to go to sea and earn his fortune there, he would have had virtually no opportunity to become the husband of a woman like Anne.

Along with ambition, Captain Wentworth has a strong sense of pride in himself and his abilities. He knows his capabilities and never doubts that he can achieve his dreams. But that pride also makes him intolerant of those who do not accept him on his own terms. Anne's rejection of his proposal eight years before the opening of the novel seriously injured his pride. He, so certain that he would succeed in his chosen profession, could not forgive her for not showing enough faith in him to accept his proposal on the basis of nothing more than his ambition. He resents the fact that she takes the advice of Lady Russell and rejects his original offer of marriage.

Wentworth's injured pride causes him to misjudge Anne throughout most of the novel. He assumes that she does not love him. He avoids talking to her with any degree of intimacy and behaves in ways that, unbeknownst to him, hurt her deeply. Only when he overhears her talking with great passion with his good friend Captain Harville about the difficulties of overcoming love does he realize that she has never stopped loving him. At that moment, he also realizes the intensity of his remaining love for her. He battles with his pride, but finally finds a way to make his feelings known to her. Upon discovering how true she has been to him in her heart throughout their time apart, Wentworth again asks Anne to marry him. This time her answer is yes.

Captain Wentworth has some difficulty understanding why Anne would accept his proposal now when she refused it eight years earlier. In true Romantic fashion, he feels that, since he is the same man that he was before, the situation between them should significantly differ. But he finally understands when Anne explains her behavior eight years before:

I must believe that I was right, much as I suffered from it, that I was perfectly right in being guided by [Lady Russell].... To me, she was in the place of a parent.... I am not saying that she did not err in her advice. It was, perhaps, one of those cases in which advice is good or bad only as the event decides.... But... I was right in submitting to her, and... if I had done otherwise, I should have suffered more in continuing the engagement than I did even in giving it up, because I should have suffered in my conscience... if I mistake not, a strong sense of duty is no bad part of a woman's portion. (211)

Anne's views are in keeping with the traditional perspective. At nineteen years of age, she was not willing to go against those people she had always trusted to guide her. To follow the advice of Lady Russell was, she believes, her duty. While Captain Wentworth had been hurt by the outcome of Anne's dedication to duty, he has to admit eight years later that it is indeed not a "bad part of a woman's portion" to have "a strong sense of duty."

Anne is also right in suggesting that Lady Russell's advice is, in this case, "good or bad only as the event decides" (211). Earning one's fortune at sea during wartime was far from guaranteed for English naval captains. Numerous English ships were sunk with their captains still on board. Still other captains never earned sufficient prize money to set up as gentlemen and marry women of quality. The fact that Captain Wentworth does, in fact, succeed at what he sets out to do demonstrates his courage, his merit, and his luck; but there was no guarantee he would even return to England, alive and healthy, let alone rich. The "event decides" in this case, that Captain Wentworth will be an excellent husband for Anne Elliot, but fate could easily have reversed that decision, a fact that Captain Wentworth refuses to consider.

Anne Elliot embodies what is best about eighteenth-century traditions in England. She is an intelligent woman who strives to behave with propriety and morality in every situation. She recognizes her position in society and appreciates it, but instead of focusing on the privileges she could expect as a result of that position, she focuses on the responsibilities of her position. When the Elliots leave the neighborhood of Kellynch, Anne is the member of the family who visits the tenant farmers and other local working-class people to bid them good-bye and make certain they will be adequately provided for while the family is away. She acts in accordance with the concept of *noblesse oblige*, a concept whereby those who have wealth, land, and power consider themselves obligated to look after those connected to them, whether by blood, by tenancy, by physical proximity, or by some other bond. Anne is the only member of the Elliot family even to recognize this responsibility, let alone to act on it.

In marriage, Anne's determination to fulfill her duties and behave with the utmost propriety in each situation will probably moderate Captain Wentworth's tendency to be intolerant of behaviors that do not fit immediately into his own belief system. Likewise, Wentworth's love of action and excitement will probably keep Anne from ignoring her own feelings and desires in an attempt to live only for duty. Together, they represent the energy, excitement, and dynamism of the coming age without giving up the ethics of duty and benevolence that have underpinned the more positive aspects of the traditional way of life in eighteenth-century England.

THEMATIC ISSUES

Persuasion is one of the dominant themes of the novel *Persuasion*. Should one allow oneself to be persuaded? Should one attempt to persuade? What are the consequences of persuading someone else or of being persuaded oneself? Those questions are some of the most important themes explored throughout the novel.

As the novel opens, Sir Walter Elliot is faced with the dilemma of having to find a way to live on less income, to "retrench" (7). His estate agent, Lady Russell, and Anne discuss among themselves the best way to accomplish the required reduction in expenses. They come up with a variety of plans, but are faced with the necessity of "persuading" Sir Walter to agree to one of those alternatives. No efficient plan of retrenchment was acceptable to Sir Walter, but he was eventually persuaded to accept a less dramatic plan, that of leasing Kellynch Hall to the Crofts while spending time in lodgings in Bath, a stylish resort town where he could maintain a lifestyle of pleasure and prosperity while, in fact, economizing.

Sir Walter's being convinced to go to Bath is only the first of many persuasions in the novel. Captain Wentworth is persuaded to frequent the Musgrove's home, to dine with them, to go shooting with Mr. Musgrove and Charles, even to participate in flirtations with the Musgrove girls. Henrietta is persuaded to accept Charles Hayter's offer of marriage. Captain Benwick is persuaded by Anne to talk about his grief and to share with her his favorite poetry. Sir Walter is persuaded to accept William Elliot's apologies for the long silence between members of their two separate branches of the family. Louisa is persuaded to marry Captain Benwick. Most importantly, Anne is persuaded by Lady Russell not to marry Wentworth prior to his earning wealth and position through his wartime activities. In a novel that emphasizes the power of the individual to achieve success through his own efforts and individual merit, the degree to which so much of what people do is based on persuasion in one form or another is somewhat surprising.

Persuasion can be a two-edged sword, as Anne Elliot infers when she claims that Lady Russell's advice to break the engagement with Wentworth eight years before may have been one of those situations in which "advice is good or bad only as the event decides" (211). Most of the attempts to persuade in *Persuasion* are, in fact, entered into with the best of motives. But whether the result of such interference into the lives of others is ultimately good, bad, or indifferent depends on the consequences. People like Lady Russell and Mr. Shepherd believe that they know better than those with less intellect, less experience, and/or less power. Sometimes they are correct, but not always. Fate can intercede, sometimes changing the situation dramatically. And sometimes persuasions backfire, one instance of which is William Elliot's attempt to persuade Mrs. Clay not to pursue Sir Walter as a marriage partner. Elliot accomplishes his goal but must face consequences that may ultimately be worse than his original fear.

The act of persuasion in Austen's novel is a dangerous game. By the end, the reader comes to believe that attempts to persuade others can be dangerous to oneself as well as to those one tries to persuade. The reader also comes to understand that being too easily persuaded by others can be a sign of weakness, but that, when the advice given is appropriate, being willing to be persuaded can also be a sign that one is willing to live according to duty and propriety. Persuasion, like advice, is often "good or bad only as the event decides" (211).

Another important thematic concern in *Persuasion* is that of selfishness vs. selflessness. Those characters like Sir Walter, Elizabeth, Mrs. Clay, and William Elliot, who focus only on their own selfish desires, are revealed to be extremely shallow characters who lack any clear sense of ethics or depth of personality. Anne Elliot, Mr. and Mrs. Musgrove, Mrs. Harville, and Captain Benwick demonstrate a selfless concern for others that often causes them to take on responsibilities that impinge upon their freedom as well as, at times, their desires.

The selfish characters in *Persuasion* are depicted as poor role models. Sir Walter, though retaining his position and his estate, is a shallow individual whose existence is stale and stagnant. His entire motivation in life is to hold onto the social position he was born to and to augment it, if possible, by association with those of even higher positions, regardless of their personalities, morals, or intellects. Thus, renewing his association with Lady Dalrymple, a boring woman who happens to be distantly related to the Elliots and who has a higher standing in society than they do, becomes his priority while in Bath. Getting to know an interesting and good man like Captain Wentworth does not appeal to him at all.

Elizabeth Elliot's focus on wealth and position and the ways she can take advantage of both causes her never to progress beyond the role of daughter to Sir Walter and mistress of Kellynch in the absence of her father's late wife. She expects to marry William Elliot, enabling her to continue in her role as mistress of Kellynch after her father's death as well, but that expectation is thwarted. Elizabeth's selfishness is of a passive nature. She expects to be granted her desires without expending any real effort. Being Sir Walter's eldest daughter seems to her to be the only prerequisite that should be necessary for the achievement of her dreams.

Mrs. Clay, on the other hand, is an active force of selfishness. After her first husband's death, she sets out to capture another husband, richer and more malleable than the first. She befriends Elizabeth, acting and saying whatever is necessary in order for Elizabeth to consider her presence indispensable. Her purpose is not, however, to be indispensable to Elizabeth. Instead, she intends to win the heart (or at least the hand) of Sir Walter Elliot. To become mistress of Kellynch is Mrs. Clay's ultimate goal.

Mr. William Elliot is cut from the same cloth as Mrs. Clay. He recognizes her game and, knowing that, if she succeeds in marrying Sir Walter, she could give him a male heir who would eliminate William's chance of ever becoming a baronet and owner of Kellynch, he sets out to disrupt her plans. To do so, he courts her himself, intending by that means to keep her away from Sir Walter. William believes, of course, that he can handle Mrs. Clay, that no matter how involved he becomes with her, she will never gain any significant control over him. By the end of the novel, he has succeeded in wooing her away from Sir Walter for good. She is "next heard of as established under [William Elliot's] protection in London" (214). Her intentions at that point clearly are to charm or otherwise coerce William Elliot into marrying her. His are to prevent such an eventuality from happening. The novel does not tell us who eventually wins. Instead Austen writes that "it is now a doubtful point whether his cunning, or hers, may finally carry the day; whether after preventing her from being the wife of Sir Walter, he may not be wheedled and caressed at last into making her the wife of Sir William" (214). The actively selfish individuals, out only for their own interests and caring not at all whether their behavior harms others, end up together, having to be constantly on guard against the machinations of each other.

Selflessness, on the other hand, is rewarded in Austen's novel. When Louisa Musgrove is seriously injured in her fall at Lyme, Mrs. Harville takes her in and insists upon nursing her back to health. The Harvilles do not stop to think of the inconveniences that having a virtual stranger living in their small home with them will present. Instead, they happily open their home to her and use as much of their energies as necessary in helping her regain her health. Louisa's parents, grateful to find Louisa in such good hands, offer to take the Harville children back to their home with them. By doing so, they not only provide a quieter household for Louisa to recover in, but they also satisfy their young charges' needs and desires as fully as they can. Through the selfless actions of both families, a friendship is established between them that will be sustained throughout their lives and quite possibly into generations to follow.

Captain Benwick displays his own brand of selfless behavior in response to Louisa's accident. She is unable to be active for a long time after the accident, and Captain Benwick, by nature a quiet man, stays by her side throughout her recovery, reading to her, talking with her, and generally keeping her mind off her physical difficulties. In order to accomplish this goal, Captain Benwick has to stop indulging his grief over the loss of Fanny Harville and focus on the needs of another person. In the process of his unselfish caretaking of Louisa, he falls in love with her and she with him. Had he not been willing to extend himself to her, even through his grief over the loss of Fanny, he would never have found the deep love that developed between them over the course of many weeks of reading and intimate conversation together.

Anne Elliot is the most selfless of all the characters in *Persuasion*. She suffers longer and more deeply than any other character in the novel, but, in the end, her happiness is perhaps the greatest of all. Anne believes in doing one's duty, whether it be helping those impoverished or ill in the neighborhood she lives in, assisting her sister with the duties of motherhood, or giving up the man she loves because the woman who stands in the place of a mother to her disapproves of the engagement. Anne continually gives up what would make her most comfortable in order to be of service to others. When Sir Walter is faced with the necessity of retrenching, Anne would prefer that they rent a cottage in the neighborhood of Kellynch while leasing out the estate. Her father and sister decide, however, to move to Bath, and, despite the fact that Anne has always detested Bath, she makes no objection to their plan. When her sister Mary asks her to stay with her to help with the children, Anne makes no objection. Mary leaves the most difficult tasks of child rearing to Anne, but she doesn't complain. She realizes that Mary's children, especially when sick, benefit more from her own quiet and efficient ways than from their mother's excited and disruptive behavior in the sickroom.

Despite the fact that Anne has never stopped loving Captain Wentworth, she never betrays those feelings to him even once until such time as she has reason to believe that he continues to love her. She is put in the position of having to watch his attentions to Henrietta and Louisa Musgrove and dreads hearing of his engagement to either one of the sisters. Yet she remains quiet about her feelings. She does not even find a confidante with whom she could release her pain. Only when she is certain beyond any doubt that Captain Wentworth has no intention of marrying either of the Musgrove women and that, in fact, he displays clear evidence of continuing to care for her, does she reveal her feelings to anyone. Her reward for all her selflessness is a life of happiness with the man she has loved since she was a teenager. She also has the satisfaction of knowing that she has behaved throughout with propriety and decorum, that she has, by her behavior, harmed no one and helped many. Such satisfaction is extremely important to a woman like Anne Elliot.

A SOCIOHISTORICAL READING OF *PERSUASION*

Novels, by their very nature, reflect the culture of which they are a part. The mores of the society are presented in the details of the story, even when they are not significant in the plot or themes of the story itself. Realistic novels, such as those Jane Austen authored, reflect the culture of their author in every aspect of their being. The social structures of her novels are the same as those of the world she lived in. As a result, much can be learned about the culture of England at the beginning of the nineteenth century by a careful examination of her novels. In *Persuasion*, we see most clearly the changing attitudes in the second decade of the century towards men who build their own lives, raising themselves from the position of their birth into positions of wealth and power in a country where wealth and power had previously been almost the exclusive territory of those who were born to it.

Persuasion presents a world in which men of motivation and ability might, through professional activity, raise both their standard of living and their social standing. Admiral Croft has, through professional activity, raised himself to a level at which he can afford to rent the estate of a baronet. He also finds himself accepted into all levels of society at Bath, though he is more interested in spending time with his fellow sailors than in courting members of the aristocracy, most of whom he finds uninteresting.

The process by which the individual can raise himself is depicted in the novel through the character of Captain Wentworth. Wentworth is a younger son of a gentleman. His father was probably a respectable gentleman, perhaps a professional man: a clergyman or a lawyer. Wentworth, in order to provide for himself, finds it necessary to pursue a profession himself. The profession he chooses is the navy.

Unlike most professional younger sons in Austen's fiction, Wentworth actively pursues a high level of success in his profession. Austen's other fictional younger sons (Edmund Bertram and Edward Ferrars, for example) display a kind of resigned acceptance of their positions, understanding the necessity of submitting to the work associated with the profession, but not striving to achieve beyond the bounds of necessity. This latter attitude towards professional activity is one held by those trained to accept the traditional values of eighteenth-century England. The attitude held by Captain Wentworth and Admiral Croft is, on the other hand, much more future-oriented.

The views of Sir Walter Elliot reveal the prejudices of a deteriorated eighteenth-century aristocracy against the idea of social advancement through the professions. He admits that the naval profession can be useful, but he finds it offensive nonetheless:

I have . . . strong grounds of objection to it. . . as being the means of bringing persons of obscure birth into undue distinction, and raising men to honours which their fathers and grandfathers never dreamt of. . . . A man is in greater danger in the navy of being insulted by the rise of one whose father, his father might have disdained to speak to . . . than in any other line. (15)

We are not to take Sir Walter's words to be our guide in evaluating those men who choose the profession of the navy. This is clear from the foolishness the baronet shows throughout the novel. But his words represent the attitude of many of his time. Those who believed that tradition should prevail, that one's social position, wealth, and power should depend on one's predecessors rather than on one's own ability and activities, tended to agree with Sir Walter.

In Austen's previous novels, even a man who raised himself by means of a profession was not depicted as self-made. In *Mansfield Park*, for instance, William Price is portrayed as being successful in his navy career as the result of the patronage of Admiral Crawford. It is clear that, had he not had the Admiral's patronage, he would probably not have received his promotion to lieutenant for quite some time. William Price is "made" by Admiral Crawford's patronage; Captain Wentworth is self-made.

The portrait Austen paints of Captain Wentworth advocates a way of life much different from that of the seventeenth- and eighteenth-century hereditary family hierarchy that, although questioned and critically examined in her earlier novels, is the basis for domestic order within them. In *Persuasion*, for the first time, Austen depicts the significance of the nineteenth-century movement towards the self-made man and a society that rewards men based on their abilities and actions rather than their birth. With *Persuasion*, Jane Austen's attitude shifts, along with that of the society she is a part of, into an acceptance of what she sees as the best qualities of Romanticism in combination with the best qualities of the world of her youth. Austen has no desire to throw out the ideals of benevolence and *noblesse oblige*, ideals she portrays prominently in her heroine, Anne Elliot, but she is prepared to marry those qualities, literally, to the qualities of dynamic ambition, hard work, and solid achievement that we see in the character of Captain Wentworth.

Bibliography

WORKS BY JANE AUSTEN

Note: All page numbers listed for Austen's novels in the text are from the editions listed below. There are many very good editions of Austen's works available, both in hardback and paperback.

FICTION

Catharine and Other Writings. Ed. Margaret Anne Doody and Douglas Murray. New York: Oxford University Press, 1993.
Emma. London: J. M. Dent and Sons, 1906.
Mansfield Park. 2 volumes. Boston: Little, Brown, 1903.
Northanger Abbey and Persuasion. London: J. M. Dent and Sons, 1906.
Pride and Prejudice. New York: Caxton House, 1900.
Sense and Sensibility. London: J. M. Dent and Sons, 1906.

COLLECTIONS OF LETTERS

Jane Austen: Selected Letters, 1796–1817. Ed. R. W. Chapman. Oxford: Oxford University Press, 1985.
Jane Austen's Letters. 3rd ed. Ed. Deirdre Le Faye. New York: Oxford University Press, 1977.

Jane Austen's Letters to Her Sister Cassandra and Others. 2nd. ed. Ed. R.W. Chapman. London: Oxford University Press, 1952.

BIOGRAPHICAL MATERIAL

Austen, Caroline. *My Aunt Jane Austen: A Memoir*. London, Jane Austen Society, 1952.

Austen-Leigh, J[ames] E[dward]. *A Memoir of Jane Austen*. London: Macmillan, 1906.

Austen-Leigh, William and Richard Arthur Austen-Leigh. *Jane Austen: Her Life and Letters, a Family Record*. 2nd ed. New York: E.P. Dutton, 1914.

Cecil, Lord David. *A Portrait of Jane Austen*. New York: Hill and Wang, 1979.

Halperin, John. *The Life of Jane Austen*. Baltimore: Johns Hopkins, 1984.

Hill, Constance. *Jane Austen: Her Homes and Her Friends*. 1902. New York: Routledge/Thoemmes Press, 1995.

Honan, Park. *Jane Austen: Her Life*. New York: St. Martins, 1987.

Le Faye, Deirdre. "Anna Lefroy's Original Memories of Jane Austen." *Review of English Studies* NS 39, 155 (August 1988): 417–21.

Tomalin, Claire. *Jane Austen: A Life*. New York: Alfred A. Knopf, 1997.

Tucker, George Holbert. *A Goodly Heritage: A History of Jane Austen's Family*. Manchester: Carcanet Press, 1983.

Wilks, Brian. *Jane Austen*. London: Hamlyn, 1978.

HISTORICAL DOCUMENTS

Blackstone, Sir William. *Commentaries of the Laws of England. Book the First*. Oxford: Oxford University Press, 1765.

Chapone, Hester, John Gregory, and Lady Pennington. *Chapone's Improvement of the Mind; Gregory's Legacy; Lady Pennington's Advice*. London: Scott and Webster, n.d.

Gisborne, Thomas. *An Enquiry Concerning Political Justice*. London, 1793. Reprinted in *Readings in English Prose of the Eighteenth Century*. Ed. Raymond Macdonald Alden. Boston: Houghton Mifflin, 1911.

Hayley, William. *A Philosophical, Historical, and Moral Essay on Old Maids*. London: T. Cadell, 1797.

Johnson, Samuel. *A Dictionary of the English Language*. London, 1755. London: Times Book Limited, 1983.

Macaulay Graham, Catherine. *Letter on Education with Observations on Religious and Metaphysical Subjects*. 1790. New York: Garland Press, 1974.

West, [Jane]. *Letters to a Young Lady, in which the Duties and Character of Women Are Considered*. 2nd ed. London, 1806.

REVIEWS AND CRITICISM

SENSE AND SENSIBILITY

Kaplan, Deborah. "Achieving Authority: Jane Austen's First Published Novel." *Nineteenth-Century Fiction* 37 (1983): 531–551.

Kaufman, David. "Law and Propriety, *Sense and Sensibility*: Austen on the Cusp of Modernity." *ELH* 59.2 (Summer 1992): 385–408.

Ruoff, Gene W. *Jane Austen's Sense and Sensibility*. New York: St. Martin's, 1992.

Smith, Phoebe A. "*Sense and Sensibility* and 'The Lady's Law': The Failure of Benevolent Paternalism." *CEA Critic* 55.3 (Spring-Summer 1993): 3–25.

Wallace, Tara Ghostal. "*Sense and Sensibility* and the Problem of Feminine Authority." *Eighteenth-Century Fiction* 4.2 (Jan. 1992): 149–163.

PRIDE AND PREJUDICE

Anderson, Walter E. "Plot, Character, Speech, and Place in *Pride and Prejudice*." *Nineteenth-Century Fiction* 30.1 (1975): 367–382.

Hirsch, Gordon. "Shame, Pride and Prejudice: Jane Austen's Psychological Sophistication." *Mosaic* 25.1 (Winter 1992): 63–78.

Morgan, Susan. "Intelligence in *Pride and Prejudice*." *Modern Philology* 73.1 (1975): 54–68.

Schneider, Matthew. Card-Playing and the Marriage Gamble in *Pride and Prejudice*." *Dalhousie Review* 73.1 (Spring 1993): 5–17.

Weinsheimer, Joel. "Chance and the Hierarchy of Marriages in *Pride and Prejudice*." In *Jane Austen*. Ed. Harold Bloom. New York: Chelsea, 1986. 13–25.

MANSFIELD PARK

Cleere, Eileen. "Reinvesting Nieces: *Mansfield Park* and the Economics of Endogamy." *Novel* 28.2 (Winter 1995): 113–130.

Giotta, Peter C. "Characterization in *Mansfield Park*: Tom Bertram and Colman's *The Heir at Law*." *Review of English Studies* 49 (1998): 466–471.

Hummel, Madeline. "Emblematic Charades and the Observant Woman in *Mansfield Park*." *Texas Studies in Literature and Language* 15 (1973): 251–65.

Palmer, Sally B. "Austen's *Mansfield Park*." *The Explicator* (Summer 1998): 181–183.

Waldron, Mary. "The Frailties of Fanny: *Mansfield Park* and the Evangelical Movement." *Eighteenth Century Fiction* 6.3 (1994): 259–282.

EMMA

Harvey, W. J. "The Plot of *Emma*." *Essays in Criticism* 17 (1967): 48–63.

Schorer, Mark. "The Humiliations of Emma Woodhouse." In *Jane Austen: A Collection of Critical Essays*. Ed. Ian Watt. NJ: Prentice-Hall, 1963. 98–111.

Sulloway, Alison G. "Emma Woodhouse and *A Vindication of the Rights of Women*." *The Wordsworth Circle* 7 (1976): 320–332.

PERSUASION

Brown, Julia Prewitt. "Private and Public in *Persuasions*." *Persuasion* (Dec. 15, 1993): 131–138.

Clausen, Christopher. "Jane Austen Changes Her Mind." *The American Scholar* 68 (1999): 89+.

Collins, K. K. "Mrs. Smith and the Morality of *Persuasion*." *Nineteenth-Century Fiction* 50 (1975): 383–397.

Hopkins, Robert. "Moral Luck and Judgment in Jane Austen's *Persuasion*." *Nineteenth-Century Literature* 42 (1987): 143–158.

Kirkham, Margaret. "Feminist Irony and the Priceless Heroine of *Mansfield Park*." In *Jane Austen: New Perspectives*. Ed. Janet Todd. New York: Holmes and Meier, 1983. 231–247.

Ruoff, Gene W. "Anne Elliot's Dowry: Reflections on the Ending of *Persuasion*." In *Jane Austen*. Ed. Harold Bloom. New York: Chelsea, 1986. 57–68.

NORTHANGER ABBEY

Axelrod, Arthur M. "Jane Austen's 'Susan' Restored." *Persuasions* (Dec. 15, 1993): 44–45.

Levine, George. "Translating the Monstrous: *Northanger Abbey*." *Nineteenth-Century Fiction* 50 (1975): 335–350.

Smith, Amy Elizabeth. "'Julias and Louisas': Austen's *Northanger Abbey* and the Sentimental Novel." *English Language Notes* 30.1 (Sept. 1992): 33–42.

OTHER SECONDARY SOURCES

Bonfield, Lloyd. *Marriage Settlements, 1601–1740: The Adoption of the Strict Settlement*. Cambridge: Cambridge University Press, 1983.

Brown, Julia Prewitt. *Jane Austen's Novels: Social Change and Literary Form*. Cambridge: Harvard University Press, 1979.

Butler, Marilyn. *Jane Austen and the War of Ideas*. Oxford: Clarendon, 1975.

———. *Romantics, Rebels and Reactionaries: English Literature and Its Background, 1760–1830*. Oxford: Oxford University Press, 1981.

Davidoff, Leonore and Catherine Hall. *Family Fortunes: Men and Women of the English Middle Class, 1780–1850*. Chicago: University of Chicago Press, 1987.

Duckworth, Alistair M. *The Improvement of the Estate: A Study of Jane Austen's Novels*. Baltimore: Johns Hopkins Press, 1971.

English, Barbara and John Saville. *Strict Settlement: A Guide for Historians*. Hull, England: University of Hull Press, 1983.

Evans, Mary. *Jane Austen and the State*. London: Tavistock Press, 1987.

Green, Katherine Sobba. *The Courtship Novel, 1740–1820. A Feminized Genre*. Lexington: University Press of Kentucky, 1991.

Harding, D. W. "Regulated Hatred: An Aspect of the Work of Jane Austen." *Scrutiny* 8 (1940): 346–362.

Hopkins, Lisa. "Jane Austen and Money." *Wordsworth Circle* 25.2 (Spring 1994): 76–78.

Hudson, Glenda. *Sibling Love and Incest in Jane Austen's Fiction*. New York: St. Martin's, 1992.

Hunter, J. Paul. *Before Novels: The Cultural Contexts of Eighteenth-Century English Fiction*. New York: W.W. Norton, 1990.

Johnson, Claudia L. *Jane Austen: Women, Politics and the Novel*. Chicago: University of Chicago Press, 1988.

Kirkham, Margaret. *Jane Austen, Feminism and Fiction*. Totawa, NJ: Barnes and Noble, 1983.

Mews, Hazel. *Frail Vessels: Woman's Role in Women's Novels from Fanny Burney to George Eliot*. London: Athlone, 1969.

Milsom, S.F.C. *Historical Foundations of the Common Law*. London: Butterworths, 1969.

Monaghan, David, ed. *Jane Austen in a Social Context*. Totowa, NJ: Barnes and Noble, 1981.

Morgan, Susan. *In the Meantime: Character and Perception in Jane Austen's Fiction*. Chicago: University of Chicago Press, 1980.

Mudrick, Marvin. *Jane Austen: Irony as Defense and Discovery*. Princeton, NJ: Princeton University Press, 1952.

Nardin, Jane. *Those Elegant Decorums: The Concept of Propriety in Jane Austen's Novels*. Albany: State University of New York Press, 1973.

Poovey, Mary. *The Proper Lady and the Woman Writer*. Chicago: University of Chicago Press, 1984.

Ruderman, Anne Crippen. *The Pleasures of Virtue: Political Thought in the Novels of Jane Austen*. Lanham, MD: Rowman and Littlefield, 1995.

Southam, B. C. *Jane Austen: The Critical Heritage*. London: Routledge and Kegan Paul, 1968.

Spring, Eileen. "The Strict Settlement: Its Role in Family History." *Economic History Review*, 2nd series, 41 (1988): 454–460.

Sulloway, Alison G. *Jane Austen and the Province of Womanhood*. Philadelphia: University of Pennsylvania Press, 1989.

Tanner, Tony. *Jane Austen*. Cambridge: Harvard University Press, 1986.

Teachman, Debra. *Understanding* Pride and Prejudice: *A Student Casebook to Issues, Sources, and Historical Documents*. Wesport, CT: Greenwood Press, 1997.

Todd, Janet, ed. *Jane Austen: New Perspectives*. New York: Holmes and Meier, 1983.

Watt, Ian, ed. *Jane Austen: A Collection of Critical Essays*. Englewood Cliffs, NJ: Prentice-Hall, 1963.

Index

About the Author

DEBRA TEACHMAN teaches English literature and composition at New Mexico State University, Alamogordo. She is also author of *Understanding Pride and Prejudice: A Student Casebook to Issues, Sources, and Historical Documents* (Greenwood 1997).